ILLUSTRATED
ATLAS OF
WORLD
HISTORY

Kingfisher Books, Grisewood & Dempsey Ltd,
Elsley House, 24–30 Great Titchfield Street,
London W1P 7AD

First published in 1991 by Kingfisher Books.
Material in this edition was previously published
in 1990 by Kingfisher Books in four separate volumes:
The Ancient World, Trade & Religion,
Exploration & Empire, and *Revolution & Technology.*

BRITISH LIBRARY CATALOGUING IN PUBLICATION DATA

Adams, Simon
    Illustrated atlas of world history.
    1. World History, Maps, atlases
    I. Title II. Briquebec, John III. Kramer, Ann
    911

ISBN 0-86272-761-8

General editor: Nicola Barber
Editor: Ann Kramer
Designer: Robert Wheeler

Maps: Eugene Fleury and Malcolm Porter
Illustrations: Kevin Maddison
Additional illustrations: Vanessa Card, Stephen Conlin
Picture research: Elaine Willis
Phototypeset by Rowland Phototypesetting Ltd,
    Bury St Edmunds, Suffolk
Printed in Hong Kong

ILLUSTRATED ATLAS OF WORLD HISTORY

Simon Adams   John Briquebec   Ann Kramer

Kingfisher Books

Contents

Introduction

This book tells the history of the world from the time when the very first peoples inhabited the Earth some 300,000 years ago, up to the present day. It traces the rise of the world's first civilizations, the growth of different cultures around the world, and moves through the development of religions, trade, industry and technology to our modern, fast-moving world. The world has changed in many ways. Thousands of years ago, different cultures arose in every part of the world. But they had little connection with each other as they were limited to the distance that people could travel. Gradually civilizations made increasing contact with each other. Some flourished, some were destroyed, but over the years human history shifted from the story of separate civilizations to the history of one, interconnected world.

This Historical Atlas is divided into four sections. The first is *The Ancient World*. This describes how the earliest people emerged in Africa and spread around place to place surviving by gathering food and hunting. Gradually, our ancestors learned how to use fire and to make tools, and then, to farm. The first farmers' settled in the Middle East, home of the first civilizations and cities. The *Ancient World* describes the great civilizations of Egypt, China, Greece, and Rome. It also describes the development of writing and language, and the rise of the world's great religions. development of writing and language, and the rise of the world's great religions.

Trade and Religion, traces human history from AD456 to 1450. It tells the story of the world from the fall of Rome to the beginning of the Reformation. It covers the break-up of the Roman and Chinese empires, the growth of the Byzantine empire, the rise of the great Islamic empire and culture. It also describes the rise of empires in America, Africa, and Asia, as well as the growth of cities and medieval culture in Europe. This section traces too the course and impact of the Black Death.

Exploration and Empire, looks at the history of the world from 1450 to 1760, from the Renaissance to the start of the Industrial Revolution. It looks at the glittering Aztec and Inca civilizations, explores the great age of exploration, and development of world-wide trade and its effects, the settlement of the Caribbean and the Americas, and the rise of empires in China and Japan. This section looks at the development of printing, the history of slavery, and the growth of science.

Finally, *Revolution and Technology* tells the story of the modern world from the Industrial Revolution to the present day. It looks at the impact of industrialism and of the great social revolutions in North America, France, Russia, and China. It covers the two world wars, and the years since 1945 including the Cold War, the rise of the nuclear age, and the growth of the environmental movement.

History is not just about dates and events. It is a story about people and how they have lived. This book takes a close look at the daily lives of people from the very beginnings of history to the present. It includes special feature pages on the rise of religion, the development of language, printing, slavery, the role of women, transport, trade, and the rise of science and technology. Using carefully chosen illustrations, maps and photographs, the *Illustrated Atlas of World History* brings history to life in a colourful and exciting fashion. Difficult words in the text are highlighted in **bold** and explained in the Glossary, while a Timeline at the end of the book provides a list of key dates.

Opposite: A section from a copy – made in the 1200s of a map which shows the world as known to the Romans.

THE ANCIENT WORLD

From the Earliest Civilizations to the Roman Empire

30,000 BC–AD 456

The Earth is Peopled

History is what people write down about the past, and the way in which it is interpreted. But to find out about life before written language was invented, about 5000 years ago, we have to rely on **archaeology**: the study of what people leave behind them – their buildings, the tools they used, the clothes they wore, their pottery and paintings. Scientists can measure very accurately when objects were made and used, so we can learn a surprising amount about the **culture** of these long-dead people – that is, the way they lived, what they believed and how they behaved.

Scientists called **anthropologists** use the remains of people themselves to show how humans developed from a group of mammals called the **Primates**, which also includes the great apes, gorillas and chimpanzees. The earliest traces of **hominids** – people-like creatures – have been found in Africa and are given the scientific name *Australopithecus* meaning 'southern ape'. The oldest-known fossil of *Australopithecus* was found in Ethiopia in 1981 and is four million years old. Modern people, whose scientific name is *Homo sapiens*, have existed for at least 300,000 years.

▲ Finding out about the past on a site in Peru. Archaeologists set out a grid so that they can locate and record accurately any 'finds' that they come across. In this way they can learn more about the people who made the things they discover.

◀ When archaeologists dig up the remains of ancient humans they usually find only **fossilized** skeletons. But the body of this man was discovered at Lindow Moss in Cheshire, England with the skin still intact, preserved by the bog in which it was found. He was murdered about 2000 years ago, perhaps as a religious sacrifice.

10

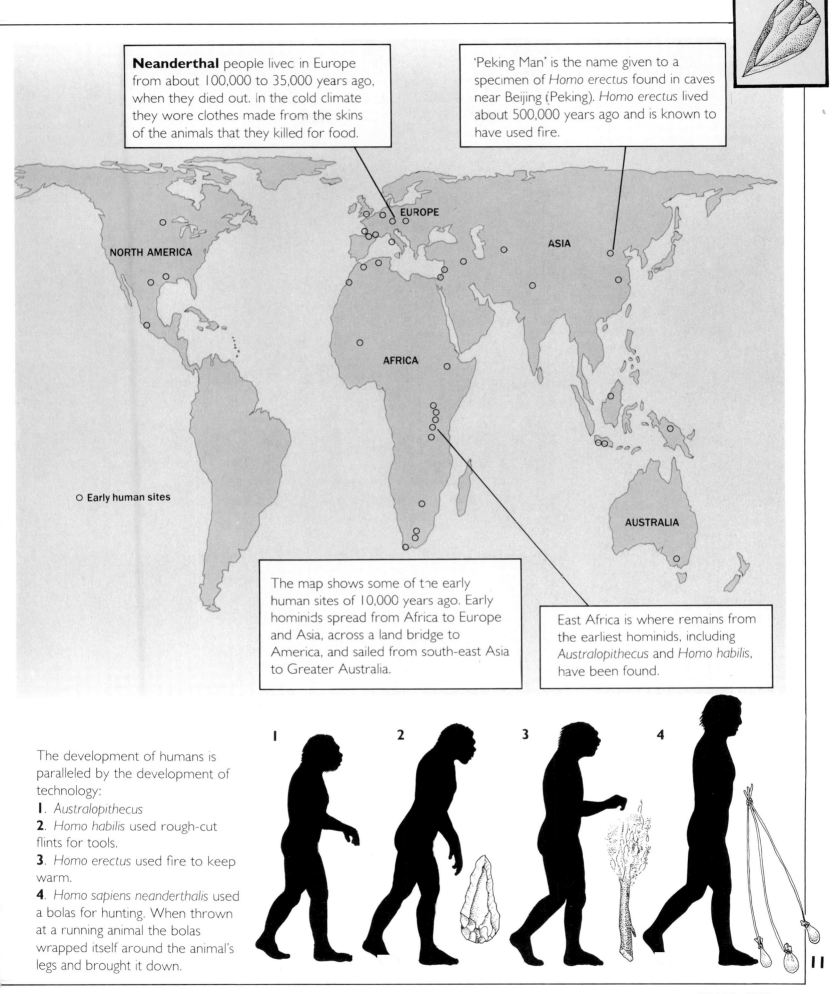

Neanderthal people lived in Europe from about 100,000 to 35,000 years ago, when they died out. In the cold climate they wore clothes made from the skins of the animals that they killed for food.

'Peking Man' is the name given to a specimen of *Homo erectus* found in caves near Beijing (Peking). *Homo erectus* lived about 500,000 years ago and is known to have used fire.

NORTH AMERICA

EUROPE

ASIA

AFRICA

AUSTRALIA

○ Early human sites

The map shows some of the early human sites of 10,000 years ago. Early hominids spread from Africa to Europe and Asia, across a land bridge to America, and sailed from south-east Asia to Greater Australia.

East Africa is where remains from the earliest hominids, including *Australopithecus* and *Homo habilis*, have been found.

The development of humans is paralleled by the development of technology:

1. *Australopithecus*

2. *Homo habilis* used rough-cut flints for tools.

3. *Homo erectus* used fire to keep warm.

4. *Homo sapiens neanderthalis* used a bolas for hunting. When thrown at a running animal the bolas wrapped itself around the animal's legs and brought it down.

1   2   3   4

11

30,000–8000BC

The ice ages

The way in which people spread around the world was affected by climate. The past million years have seen a series of **glacials** (ice ages) with warmer spells, called **interglacials**, in between. At the height of the glacials ice sheets covered northern Europe, Asia and north America and made it too cold for human settlement. But during the warmer interglacials people began slowly to adapt to the colder temperatures farther north, by finding shelter and making fire, tools and clothes. The first people to survive the colder climate of western Europe were the Neanderthals – so called because their remains were first found in the Neander Valley (*Tal*) in West Germany. They lived between 100,000 and 35,000 years ago on areas of land bordering the great glaciers.

The ice that covered the land during the glacials took water from the seas and oceans, and as a result the sea level fell by several metres. This meant that land which had been covered by water was exposed, and people could migrate across **land bridges** to new areas. So the first people to reach America probably trekked from Siberia to Alaska about 40,000 years ago. In south-east Asia people went, probably by raft, across what were then very shallow seas to New Guinea, and from there travelled on foot over a land bridge to Australia where they settled at least 50,000 years ago.

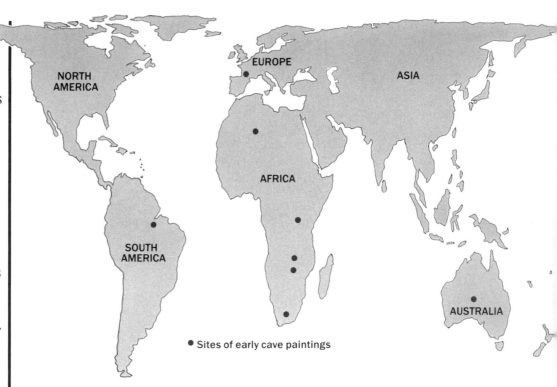

▲ The map shows where early cave and rock paintings have been found. *Homo sapiens* painted them between 35,000 and 10,000 years ago. It is thought that the animal drawings may have been part of a magical ritual connected with hunting.

▼ Part of a wall-painting discovered in a cave in Lascaux, France. The animals on this wall were painted between 19,000 and 18,000 years ago. The oxen have been drawn in black outline; the horses and deer have been filled in with a colour.

▼ This carving of a female figure holding a bison's horn was found in a cave at Laussel, France. It is between 30,000 and 15,000 years old. Several figures like this have been found in France and southern USSR. They are often called 'Venuses' because they are thought to represent mother-goddesses.

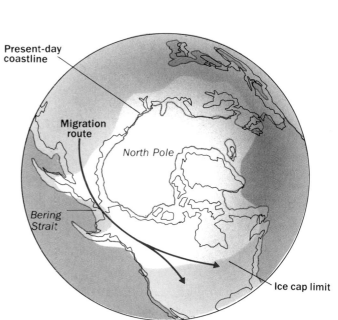

The map shows the southernmost limit reached by the ice cap in the last ice age (the Würm period). During the ice age a huge amount of water was frozen into the ice cap: in places the ice cap was 3000 metres thick. As a result the level of the world's oceans fell by more than 90 metres and there were land bridges in many places where there is now sea. Animals migrated across these land bridges, followed by the humans who hunted them. In this way early humans reached America.

◄ At first tools were made by rubbing two stones together to produce an edge on one. But using a piece of bone or stone to press flakes off a flint meant that a greater variety of tools could be produced.

1. A knife-like blade
2. A borer
3. A point

The Fertile Crescent and its Neighbours

The hunter-gatherers

The people who roamed the Earth 500,000 years ago hunted animals and gathered whatever nuts, fruits, and other vegetable matter they could find for food. When the supply of food in one place ran out, or when the herds of animals moved on, the people had to move too. Collecting or catching enough food to stay alive took up everybody's time.

The first farmers

What changed people's lives, over many generations, was the gradual development of **agriculture**. Slowly people discovered that certain plants could be grown or cultivated to provide crops, and certain animals could be protected or domesticated to provide meat, milk, hides or wool. Gradually many people began to rely on the steady supply of food from their crops and animals, and instead of moving from place to place to gather their food, they started to settle in fertile areas of land.

Some of the earliest farmers settled, nearly 10,000 years ago, in what is often called the 'Fertile Crescent'. This was an area of land which was well watered by the Tigris, Euphrates and Nile Rivers. Here people grew wild wheat and wild barley, and kept goats, sheep, pigs and cattle.

▲ Without water crops cannot grow, so a system of watering cultivated land, or **irrigation**, is very important. Different methods were used by different peoples. In this picture the ox is turning a wheel to raise pots of water from a larger channel to a smaller one.

► This cave painting shows a goat, one of the first animals to be domesticated and kept for its milk.

◄ The first grains to be cultivated were various types of wheat (**1**) and barley (**2**). The early farmers harvested wild grains and then sowed the seeds they obtained, watering them and fertilizing them to give fatter seed grains.

14

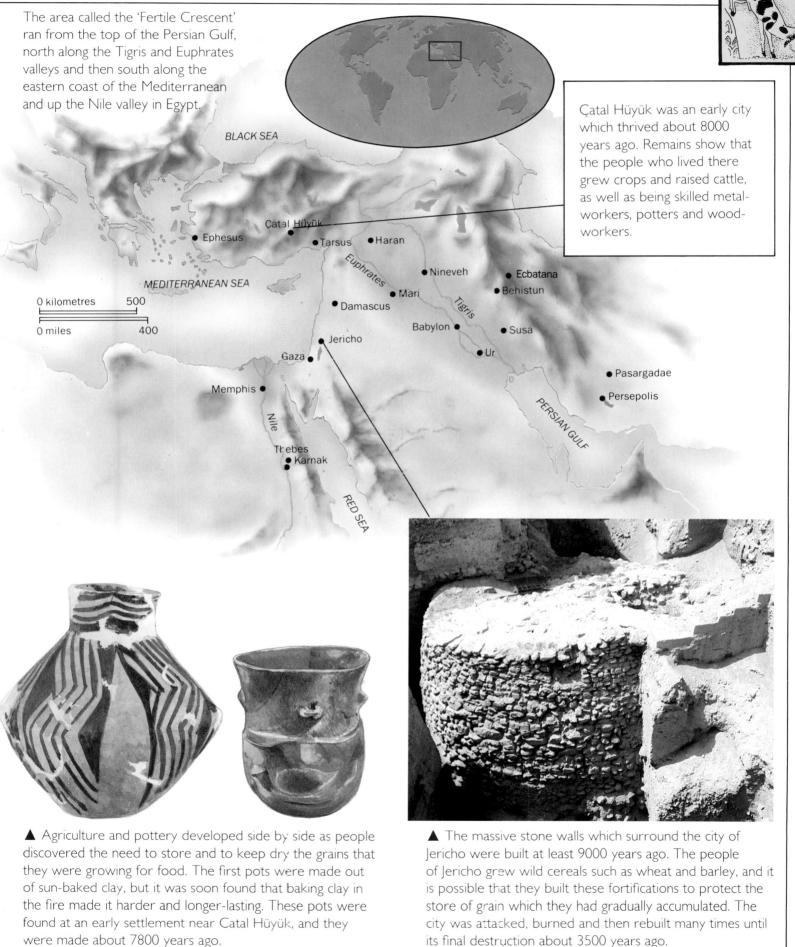

The area called the 'Fertile Crescent' ran from the top of the Persian Gulf, north along the Tigris and Euphrates valleys and then south along the eastern coast of the Mediterranean and up the Nile valley in Egypt.

BLACK SEA

MEDITERRANEAN SEA

Ephesus

Çatal Hüyük

Tarsus · Haran

Euphrates

Nineveh · Ecbatana

Mari · Behistun

Damascus

Tigris

Babylon · Susa

Jericho

Gaza

Ur

Memphis

Pasargadae

Persepolis

PERSIAN GULF

Nile

Thebes

Karnak

RED SEA

0 kilometres 500
0 miles 400

Çatal Hüyük was an early city which thrived about 8000 years ago. Remains show that the people who lived there grew crops and raised cattle, as well as being skilled metal-workers, potters and wood-workers.

▲ Agriculture and pottery developed side by side as people discovered the need to store and to keep dry the grains that they were growing for food. The first pots were made out of sun-baked clay, but it was soon found that baking clay in the fire made it harder and longer-lasting. These pots were found at an early settlement near Çatal Hüyük, and they were made about 7800 years ago.

▲ The massive stone walls which surround the city of Jericho were built at least 9000 years ago. The people of Jericho grew wild cereals such as wheat and barley, and it is possible that they built these fortifications to protect the store of grain which they had gradually accumulated. The city was attacked, burned and then rebuilt many times until its final destruction about 3500 years ago.

15

The first civilizations

After many generations settlements grew and became established, in some areas people began to co-ordinate and organize their beliefs, **trade** and government: and as a result the first **civilizations** emerged.

The earliest civilizations of the Fertile Crescent were in Mesopotamia, the land between the Tigris and the Euphrates Rivers. The first people to settle in Mesopotamia were the Sumerians. After about 3500BC they established centres of civilization in towns and cities, called 'city-states'. In each of these city-states was found a royal palace, a temple tower (**ziggurat**) and an administrative centre, around which were houses, and beyond them the fields and marshlands of the farmers. One of these city-states, Ur, became very powerful because of its trade: cloth and ready-made clothes were produced in the city's workshops and exchanged for copper, gold, ivory and timber.

Around 2000BC the power of Ur was weakened, and a **nomadic** people from the north, the Amorites, took over the land where the Tigris and the Euphrates converge and established a centre called Babylon. However Babylonia was conquered by the Assyrians, a warlike nation from the city-state of Assur, with a trained and organized army, skilled horsemen, and weapons made from **bronze** and iron.

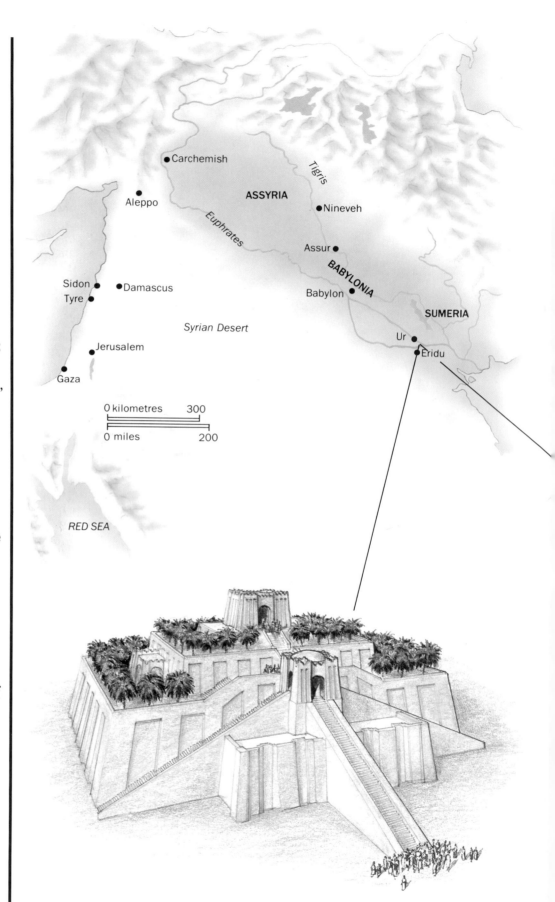

▲ A reconstruction of the ziggurat at Ur. On the top was a temple where the king performed religious rites and sacrifices with the high priestess of Ur. It was built of sun-baked, clay bricks and it may have been decorated with glazed tiles (not shown here). It was finished in about 2100BC.

16

▲ Part of the impression from a limestone cylinder **seal** made in Mesopotamia between 5500 and 5000 years ago. Seals were used to identify property. The upper part of the impression shows some cattle; below is a byre (shelter for animals).

▲ The Marsh Arabs of southern Iraq still build and live in reed houses, just as the farmers in the marshlands of Mesopotamia did. The houses are similar in construction to the byre shown on the seal (*above, left*).

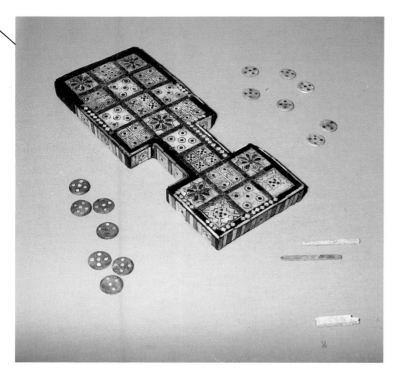

▲ A board game, complete with dice and counters, made and used in Ur about 4500 years ago. The Mesopotamians were skilled mathematicians; from them we inherit the method of dividing up time into 60 seconds, minutes and hours, and a circle into 360 degrees.

Mesopotamia
*c.*8000BC: first development of agriculture.
*c.*3500BC: the Sumerians begin to develop their civilization.
*c.*3200BC: earliest writing.
2800BC: the first Semitic people settle in Mesopotamia.
2360BC: Akkadian Empire founded by Sargon.
1792–1750BC: rule of Hammurabi, king of Babylon.
*c.*1750BC: rise of Babylonian Empire.
*c.*721–705BC Assyrian Empire at height of its power.
689BC: Babylon destroyed by Assyrians.
539BC Nabonidus, last king of Babylonia, surrenders to Cyrus the Second of Persia.

The Ancient Egyptians

Like the people of Mesopotamia, the Ancient Egyptians established their settlements on fertile land along a river, the river Nile, more than 5000 years ago. There were two **kingdoms** – Lower Egypt in the delta area at the mouth of the Nile, and Upper Egypt in the south, but these were united in 3200BC by the **Pharaoh** (king) Menes, who was the first in a line of Pharaohs who ruled Egypt for the next 2500 years. Whereas the various kingdoms of Mesopotamia, based around city-states, remained relatively small, the kingdom of Egypt flourished under one rule, with a single system governing the whole land.

At the top of this system was the Pharaoh. He was considered to be a god, and commanded the service and goods of all his subjects. The belief that, as gods, the Pharaohs continued to live after death led to the building of the Pyramids. In these huge tombs the Pharaohs were buried with everything they might need in the afterlife, including food. The immense power that the Pharaohs wielded over their people is shown by the time, the number of workers and the wealth needed to build these tombs.

Egyptian farmers

At the other end of the social system were the peasant farmers who worked in the fields. Egyptian agriculture relied on the annual flooding of the Nile River which, when the

The fertile part of Egypt was a narrow strip on either side of the Nile. Memphis was the country's capital until around 2000BC. After that Thebes became the capital.

▼ A model of a boat found in an Egyptian tomb. Rich Egyptians equipped their tombs with all the household objects, such as beds, pots, jewellery, toys and tools, which they needed for the afterlife. Most tombs also had one of these boats for the final journey up the Nile. This model shows the owner of the boat squatting before the mast, with a pilot in the bows and the crew working the sail.

▼ A section through the Great Pyramid at Giza, near Cairo, the largest of the Pyramids. It was constructed with 2,300,000 blocks of stone, each weighing an average of 2½ tonnes. Some of the stone was quarried nearby, but some of it was brought by river from Aswan and dragged on rollers from the river's edge. The Ancient Greek historian, Herodotus, records that 100,000 people toiled for 20 years to build it as a tomb for Pharaoh Khufu, who died in 2567BC.

chamber

grand gallery

Queen's chamber

entrance

▲ A wall-painting from the tomb of Menna at Thebes.

▲ Scenes from a modern reconstruction of an Egyptian village. The people who worked in the fields were hardly paid enough to live on, and a large percentage of the wheat harvest was taken away in tax.

Top Winnowing: trampled ears of grain are picked up in flat wooden scoops and tossed high into the air to separate the chaff (which blows away) from the wheat (which falls to the ground).
Below Harvested grain is carried from the field in large baskets.

► Egyptian men wore a simple linen kilt, knotted around the waist. It was sometimes ornamented with pleating at the front. Official and ceremonial dress was more complicated – for example priests wore leopard skins.

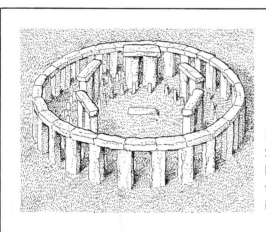

Did you know that Stonehenge in England was begun at about the same time as the Great Pyramid in Egypt?

19

water-level had subsided, left behind it fertile silt in which crops such as wheat, barley and flax could be grown. Wheat and barley were used to make bread and beer, and flax provided the linen with which the Egyptians made most of their clothes. Meat was a luxury for most Ancient Egyptians, but cattle were reared for their dairy produce, as beasts of burden and for ritual slaughter.

Egyptian people
In between these two extremes were many levels of Egyptian society such as the **viziers** and supervisors close to the Pharaoh at court, priests in the temples, merchants and craftspeople. Scribes were particularly important because they oversaw the harvest and recorded the yield of the crops; they also wrote down the history of their times and inscriptions glorifying Egyptian victories in war.

The population of Ancient Egypt was spread among the towns and small villages along the Nile. The most important settlements were the royal cities chosen by the Pharaohs such as Memphis and Thebes: next in importance were the *nome* (provincial) centres, which were local centres for administration and taxation.

All the buildings except, of course, the Pyramids and some of the temples which were built of stone, were made of unbaked mud-brick – a mixture of Nile mud and straw shaped in a wooden mould and left to dry in the sun.

▲ The Egyptians worshipped many gods and goddesses and they also believed in magic to guard against evils. This magic wand, made of hippopotamus ivory, was used to protect the owner against poisonous creatures at night.

◄ When the Pharaoh died his body was preserved by a process called mummification in order for it to continue on its journey in the afterlife. The body was swathed in bandages and enclosed in a highly-decorated mummy-case like the one shown here. Later, rich Egyptians also received this treatment.

▼ This tomb model of a man shows him filtering a fermented mixture to make beer. Beer was the main drink in Egypt. It was made from barley and stored in beer jars.

The Spread of Writing

As civilizations emerged and trade developed people began to record information by writing it down. The first writing we know of comes from Mesopotamia as early as 3200BC. Here the Sumerians drew little pictures on clay tablets, probably in order to keep records and accounts of their goods for trading. Gradually over the next 200 years these 'pictograms' were replaced by patterns made by a chopped-off reed on soft clay: each pattern stood for a sound or syllable. This type of writing is called cuneiform (meaning wedge-shaped). It lasted from about 3000BC to AD75, several centuries longer than our own writing has been in use!

Although they knew of cuneiform, the Egyptians developed their own more elaborate picture-writing called 'hieroglyphs'. Like the Sumerians the Egyptians gradually developed a system in which their pictograms stood for sounds rather than things. However, the Egyptians also invented a new and more convenient material on which to write – sheets of papyrus made from the papyrus reed, from which comes our word 'paper'.

The first surviving specimens of Chinese writing were found on the oracle bones of the Shang dynasty (*see page 23*). Over 2000 different characters have been found on these bones and it is obvious that writing was already well developed in China by this time. The Chinese language developed in a completely different way from the western languages, using the shapes of characters to represent things and ideas, not syllables or sounds.

▲ Egyptian hieroglyphs: some of the signs have the value of one letter of our alphabet, others represent two letters or more.

◀ Writing on a soft clay tablet with a reed pen

Cuneiform

Chinese characters

Indus valley glyphs

Egyptian hieroglyphs

The Persians

The last of the early civilizations of this region was in Persia (Iran). Two nomadic tribes, the Medes and the Persians, moved southwards from the area which is now southern USSR about 2900 years ago. In 549BC a Persian king, Cyrus the Great, conquered the Medes and set about creating a huge **empire**. The Persians were good riders and they used iron weapons. Within only 30 years they had expanded their empire to cover the whole of Mesopotamia, Anatolia (Turkey), the eastern Mediterranean and what are now Pakistan and Afghanistan.

However, it was left to a later Persian king, Darius the Great, to devise a system of government which would hold together this huge empire. The Empire was divided into 23 (later 31) administrative regions, called *satrapies*, each with a governor (*satrap*) who controlled a region, but who also had to make gifts of cereals and other produce to the Persian king. Roads were built, including the Royal Road, to link together the various parts of the Empire. They were also used for trade – traders transported and sold raw materials, clothes, carpets and spices. In 520BC Darius introduced a standardized currency to be used throughout the Empire which also encouraged trade.

The Persian Empire flourished until 331BC when it was conquered by the Greek, Alexander the Great of Macedonia.

▲ This tiny gold model of a Persian chariot is part of the 'Oxus treasure' found in Afghanistan. It shows the kind of vehicle in which Persian nobles travelled on business along the roads of the Empire. The Persians were skilled craftspeople, renowned for their fine work in gold and silver.

Both these impressions were taken from seals which were rolled across moist clay to produce signatures to identify property.

▲ This seal was probably the property of one of Darius's highest officials, and shows the king in his chariot, hunting lions.

◄ The ordinary people of the Empire rarely appeared on seals. This one shows a man ploughing with his team of oxen.

Extent of Persian Empire under Darius I

The Persian Empire reached its greatest size and power in about 500BC, when it was ruled by Darius the First. Susa was its administrative capital, Parsagadae its coronation city and Persepolis its centre of state.

▶ An aerial view of the ruins of Persepolis as they stand today in southern Iran. Darius the First ordered the start of building work in 520BC. Persepolis was only used by the 'King of Kings' and his court once a year during New Year, when tribute was brought to him by the peoples of his Empire.

▶ Assyrians bearing tribute to the 'King of Kings' at the New Year ceremony. They bring dressed animal skins and a pair of rams chosen from their flocks.

23

Civilizations of Eastern and Southern Asia

Ancient China

The earliest civilizations of Ancient China grew up on the banks of its three largest rivers: the Huang He (Yellow River), the Chang Jiang (Yangtse) and the Xi Jiang (West River). Like the peoples of the Fertile Crescent, the Chinese farmers relied on the rivers for water to grow their crops, and for transport, but devastating floods were always a threat. There was also the danger of invasion from the north by the Xiung-Nu (Huns or Mongols). As a result the building of waterworks, and of defences against human attacks were important features of China's early history.

The Shang

The first **dynasty**, or ruling family, of which we are certain was called the Shang. Their capital city seems to have been moved – maybe as a result of both floods and invasions. However excavations at one of the cities, An-yang, revealed wooden houses in which most people lived, as well as palaces, store rooms and tombs of the kings and people of rank.

People of the Shang Dynasty grew millet, wheat and some rice and kept domesticated animals such as cattle, pigs, sheep, dogs and chicken. Silk was already an important

▲ A reconstruction of an early Chinese house of about 2000BC. It probably housed one family. The roof was supported by wooden uprights, and traces of such uprights have been found by archaeologists excavating sites near the Huang He (Yellow River) in northern China.

▶ A pottery model of a watch-tower made around AD100. This model was made for the tomb of a wealthy person in the Han period.

Ancient China

c.1500BC: Shang Dynasty (Bronze Age culture).
1027BC: Chou Dynasty.
c.650BC: introduction of iron working.
551BC: Confucius born.
221BC: Ch'in Dynasty (first united empire).
202BC–AD220: Han Dynasty (rise of Confucianism).
c.112BC: opening of 'Silk Road' linking China to the West.
50BC–AD50: Buddhism introduced from India.
AD220–587: Six Dynasties period.

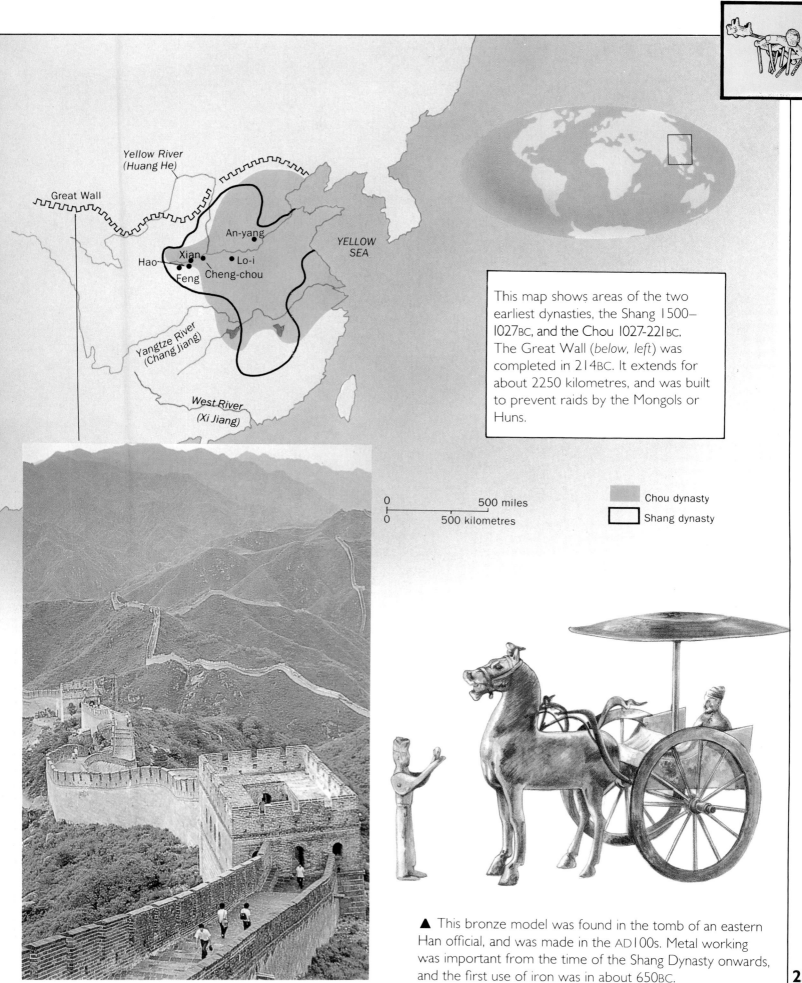

Yellow River
(Huang He)

Great Wall

An-yang

Xian
Hao
Feng
Cheng-chou
Lo-i

YELLOW
SEA

Yangtze River
(Chang Jiang)

West River
(Xi Jiang)

This map shows areas of the two earliest dynasties, the Shang 1500–1027BC, and the Chou 1027-221BC. The Great Wall (*below, left*) was completed in 214BC. It extends for about 2250 kilometres, and was built to prevent raids by the Mongols or Huns.

0 ——— 500 miles
0 ——— 500 kilometres

Chou dynasty
Shang dynasty

▲ This bronze model was found in the tomb of an eastern Han official, and was made in the AD100s. Metal working was important from the time of the Shang Dynasty onwards, and the first use of iron was in about 650BC.

cloth, but it was worn only by the rich – ordinary people wore linen or cotton.

The Dynasty came to an end when nomadic groups from the west took over, establishing the Chou Dynasty. They introduced the working of iron (in about 650BC), and whereas the Shang had used metal – usually bronze – only for ornamental purposes, now iron was used for weapons and for agricultural tools such as ploughs. This made cultivation much easier.

The Ch'in Dynasty

In 221BC a Ch'in king, Shih Huang Ti, pronounced himself Emperor and founded the Ch'in Dynasty. He unified his vast empire by standardizing weights and measures, introducing a uniform coinage, and by improving the network of roads and canals.

Nineteen years later the Ch'in Dynasty was succeeded by the Han Dynasty which ruled – with a short interruption – until AD220.

Japan

The development of civilizations was slower in Japan, mainly because of this island country's isolation. Fishing provided much of the food needed and the early Japanese, the Jomon, also cultivated grains, such as rice, and kept domestic animals. After about 100BC the Yayoi culture arose. Its people used bronze and iron to make decorative objects, but still used stone knives and simple wooden containers.

▲ The excavated tomb of Shih Huang Ti near the village of Xian in Shaanxi province. Thousands of life-size pottery figures and horses have been found guarding the tomb of the Emperor. The faces of the figures and horses are all different and may be portraits of actual people and animals.

▼ A reconstruction of the Izumo shrine in Japan, a temple of the Shinto religion. Seasonal ceremonies were held here to ensure good crops, fertility and health.

Did you know that since ancient times the Chinese have used bones as oracles, to try to foretell the future? Questions to the gods were carved onto the bones. When the bones were heated cracks appeared across the written characters and gave the gods' answers.

26

Religions and Beliefs in Eastern Asia

Three of the world's main religions and beliefs began in eastern Asia: Hinduism, Buddhism and Confucianism.

Hinduism

Hinduism is the world's oldest surviving religion and is still the main religion of India. It is not known exactly when and where it began, but the origins of Hinduism lie in the religion of the Aryan people who settled northern India from 1500BC onwards (see page 26).

Archaeologists know little about these people but what they do know has been learned from their literature which was passed down by word of mouth for many centuries. The most important early work of this literature was the *Rig-Veda* which became a holy book for all Hindus. The *Rig-Veda* is a collection of hymns which were originally chanted by the Brahmans or priests at sacrifices. It was not written down until AD1300.

The three most important Hindu gods are Brahma, creator of the Universe, Vishnu, who preserves the Universe, and Shiva who destroys it.

Buddhism

Buddhism also originated in northern India. It was founded by a prince called Siddhartha Gautama who was born in 563BC to a life of wealth and luxury. When he was 29 he left his family and rejected his comfortable life. Dressed as a beggar he wandered from place to place. Starting from the traditional teaching of the Hindu Brahmans he rejected their ritual and sacrifice and instead began to teach a method of disciplining both mind and body in order to attain *Nirvana*, a state of perfect peace and happiness. He was called Buddha, 'the Enlightened One'.

Confucianism

Confucianism is a way of life and moral behaviour rather than a religion. It is based on the teachings of a Chinese wise man who lived from 551 to 479BC. He was called Kung Fu-tzu which was translated into Latin as Confucius. As a young man he worked as an administrator for a prince, but he withdrew from active life and began to meditate on questions of right and wrong. His 'system' was that people's lives should be ruled by a principle of order: doing good meant finding your place in that order and respecting the places of other people and things in it.

The teachings of Confucius were adopted by the rulers of the Chinese empire as the official philosophy; they also spread to Korea and Japan.

▼ There are many statues and carvings of the Buddha but none are from his own time.

▲ The teachings of Confucius influenced the development of Chinese civilization for two thousand years.

The Indus valley civilizations

The early peoples of India inhabited sites around the Indus and Ganges Rivers, but the first civilization to emerge was in the Indus valley in about 2500BC.

The two largest cities of the Indus valley civilization were Mohenjo-daro and Harappa. At the centre of both was an artificial mound or **citadel**, with a large well-ventilated granary in which grain was stored. At Mohenjo-daro there was also a bath-house, with cells and private baths surrounding a large bath which may have been used by priests. Beyond the citadel the workers' houses were built in well-planned rows, with streets crossing at right-angles and a system of drains and sewers. The houses were built around a courtyard with several rooms, a well and a toilet. All of the buildings were made with bricks, baked in wood-fired ovens.

The huge granaries at Harappa and Mohenjo-daro suggest that the livelihood of the Indus valley people was based on farming – wheat and barley being the main crops. They also traded goods, such as cotton, probably with the peoples farther west in Mesopotamia.

The Indus civilization seems to have ended quite suddenly in about 1500BC, possibly when its cities were attacked by **Aryan** invaders from the north. No single civilization took its place until the Mauryan Empire emerged in central India in about 320BC.

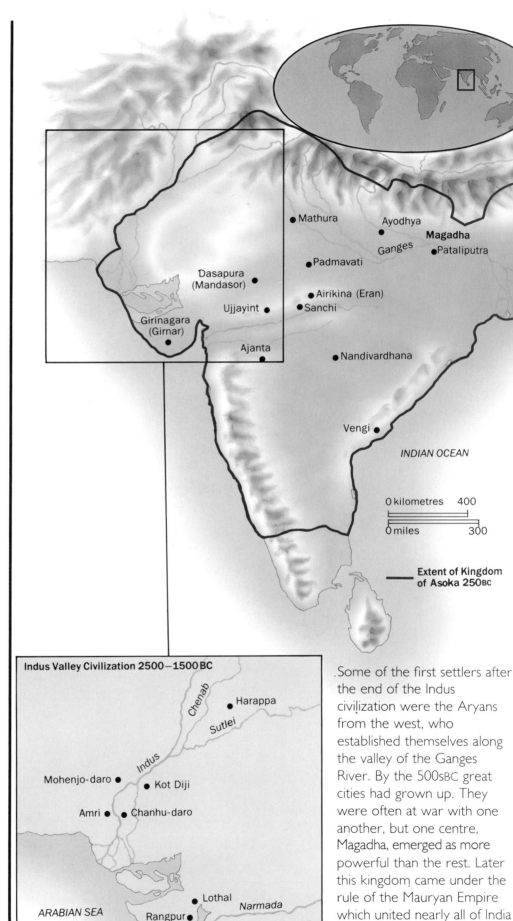

Indus Valley Civilization 2500–1500 BC

Some of the first settlers after the end of the Indus civilization were the Aryans from the west, who established themselves along the valley of the Ganges River. By the 500sBC great cities had grown up. They were often at war with one another, but one centre, Magadha, emerged as more powerful than the rest. Later this kingdom came under the rule of the Mauryan Empire which united nearly all of India under its greatest emperor, Asoka (273–232BC).

► The impressive ruins of the city of Mohenjo-daro. The buildings were carefully planned out on a grid design, and built with **kiln**-baked bricks. These bricks were of such good quality that many of them were taken away and used in the AD1800s to build railway embankments.

▼ Brick-lined shafts like this are found in the courtyards of many of the houses in Mohenjo-daro. They may have been wells or storage places for vases or jars.

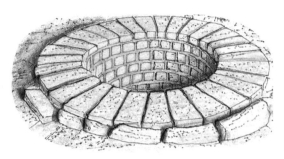

▼ Over 1200 of these seals have been found in the ruins of Mohenjo–daro. They were used by merchants to stamp bales and other property. Many of them have animal designs and show the great variety of wild animals known to the Indus valley people: elephants, tigers, rhinoceroses, antelopes, crocodiles and humped bulls.

◄ This **terracotta** statuette of a mother-goddess figure was found at Mohenjo-daro. She is wearing a loincloth and jewellery.

Ancient India
c.2500BC: Indus valley civilization begins to emerge.
c.1500BC: collapse of Indus valley civilization.
c.1500BC: Aryans settle in northern India and ? destroy Indus valley civilization.
c.800BC: Aryan settlement expands southwards.
563BC: birth of the Buddha.
327BC: Alexander the Great dies.
c.320BC: Mauryan Empire founded in northern India.

Civilizations of Europe and the Mediterranean

The civilizations that succeeded those of Mesopotamia and Egypt grew up around the shores of the Mediterranean Sea.

The Israelites

The Israelites were a **Semitic** people related to both the Babylonians and the Assyrians. They migrated to Palestine in about 2000BC, and after a period of exile in Egypt, returned to Palestine. Here, under King David, they set up a kingdom, with its capital at Jerusalem. Later, Palestine was split into two hostile kingdoms, Israel and Judah.

The Phoenicians

From 1200BC the Phoenicians established themselves along the eastern shore of the Mediterranean, where they cultivated corn, barley, olives, vines and figs. Their main centres were the ports along the coast, such as Tyre and Sidon, from where they sailed all over the Mediterranean, trading goods – timber, glassware, metalwork and ivory. In time they **colonized** much of the Mediterranean shore, the largest and most famous colony being Carthage.

One of the Phoenicians' most important exports was the purple cloth which gives them their name (Phoenicia comes from the Greek *phoinos*

▲ Masada is a natural rock fortress near the Dead Sea. It was developed by Herod the Great, king of Judea, as a fort with storehouses, baths, a synagogue (meeting place), two palaces and enough space in the centre to grow some crops. In AD72–73 a group of patriotic Jews (Zealots) made a final stand at Masada against the Romans.

The Hebrew kingdoms of Israel and Judah (later Judea) grew up in the region between the river Jordan and the Mediterranean Sea.

2000BC–AD456

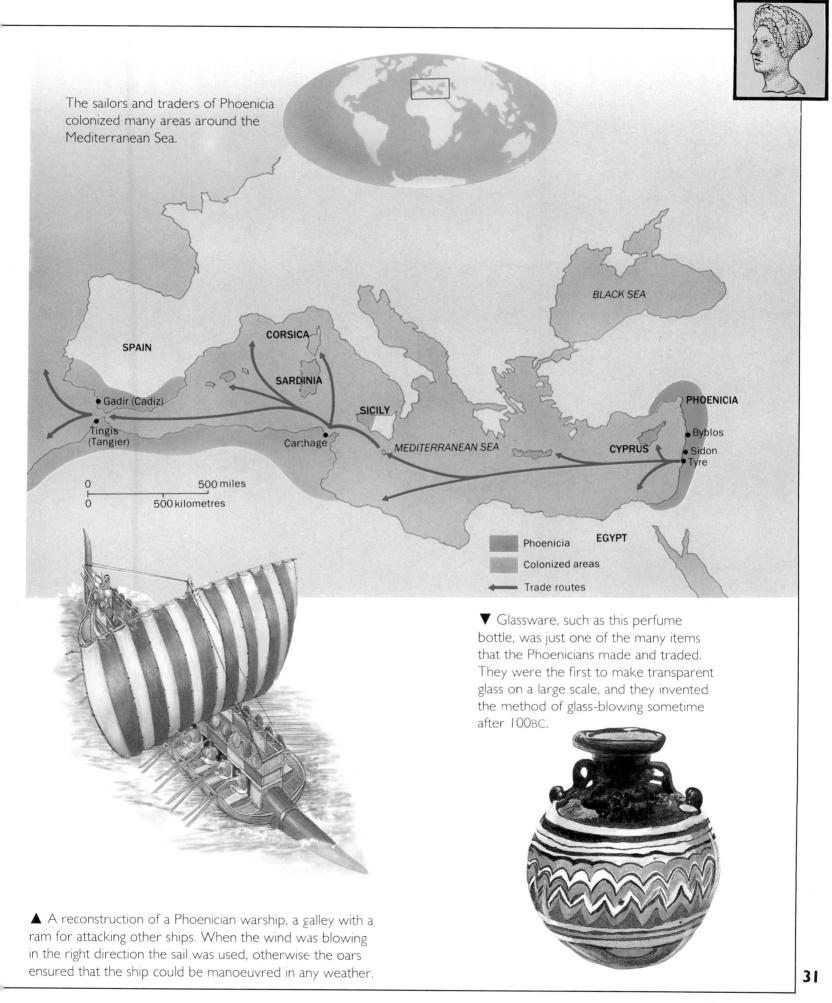

The sailors and traders of Phoenicia colonized many areas around the Mediterranean Sea.

BLACK SEA

SPAIN

CORSICA

SARDINIA

SICILY

PHOENICIA

Gadir (Cadiz)

Tingis (Tangier)

Carthage

MEDITERRANEAN SEA

CYPRUS

Byblos

Sidon

Tyre

0   500 miles
0   500 kilometres

EGYPT

Phoenicia

Colonized areas

Trade routes

▼ Glassware, such as this perfume bottle, was just one of the many items that the Phoenicians made and traded. They were the first to make transparent glass on a large scale, and they invented the method of glass-blowing sometime after 100BC.

▲ A reconstruction of a Phoenician warship, a galley with a ram for attacking other ships. When the wind was blowing in the right direction the sail was used, otherwise the oars ensured that the ship could be manoeuvred in any weather.

meaning purple). The dye for the cloth was made from a substance produced from shellfish. The vivid purple colour of the cloth became a symbol of authority in the Roman Empire.

Minos and Mycenae

The first European civilization was established on the island of Crete after about 2000BC. The Minoan civilization was named after its legendary king, Minos. The Minoans built several large cities which were connected by a network of roads. Each of these cities centred around a palace, the largest and grandest being at Knossos where there were royal apartments for the king and queen, rooms for religious rites, workshops for the skilled Minoan craftspeople, and a 'schoolroom' where pupils learned to read and write in order to become scribes.

The brilliant Minoan civilization came to an end suddenly in about 1450BC. Whether it was destroyed by an earthquake or taken over by the Mycenean Greeks is not certain.

The Mycenean Greeks established a civilization in south-east Greece at the same time as the Minoans, and were at first influenced by them. However, the Myceneans were more warlike; their cities were built like fortresses and they accumulated wealth not only by trade but also by plundering and raiding. They traded around the Mediterranean, importing copper and tin to make bronze, as well as

▼ A death mask of beaten gold from a tomb at Mycenae. When it was first found it was described as the mask of the legendary king Agamemnon. The Myceneans buried their kings and nobles in shaft graves, sunk vertically into solid rock. Beside the bodies they laid objects of bronze, gold, ivory, pottery and silver. Later tombs were made by tunnelling into hillsides.

▼ A room in the palace at Knossos showing some of the frescoes which cover the walls of the palace.

▼ The ruins of the Parthenon in Athens. The Parthenon was built between 447 and 438BC and it was designed to impress by its size and splendour. Inside, the temple housed a finely-worked statue in gold and ivory of the patron goddess of the city, Athene. There was an altar outside at which people worshipped, and where sacrifices were possibly made.

▲ This little bronze statue of a girl athlete from Sparta is part of a lid of a vase found in Yugoslavia. Whereas Athenian girls were kept at home and taught how to be good housewives, girls from the city-state of Sparta were encouraged to lead much freer lives.

0   300 kilometres

0   200 miles

MACEDONIA

ITALY

Troy

GREECE Lemnos

THESSALY ASIA MINOR

     AEGEAN
BOIOTIA   SEA
  ● Delphi

IONIAN Corinth● ● Athens
SEA Olympia ●
    Mycenae

SICILY PELOPONNESE

   ● Sparta

       Rhodes

     Santorini

MEDITERRANEAN SEA   CYPRUS

    Knossos

   CRETE

precious stones and metals. In exchange they exported bronze weapons, jewellery, olive oil, wine and wool.

Athenians and Spartans

The importance of the Myceneans decreased after about 1100BC. In the mountainous Greek countryside city-states gradually grew up on the small plains between the mountains. Communication was often difficult between the city-states, so each small state developed separately and had its own government and laws, and often its own army, currency, weights and measures. Each city-state was governed by an **aristocratic** family. Around the central city or *polis* of each state were the villages and farms of the ordinary people where they grew corn, olives and vegetables, and reared goats for cheese and milk.

Two of these city-states grew in importance: Sparta and Athens. The Athenians developed the idea of **democracy**, by which they meant that the people took a direct part in government. But 'the people' included only the Athenian male **citizens**: women, slaves and people who were not Athenians had no political rights.

In 481BC Sparta and Athens united to fight a war against a common enemy – Persian invaders. But later in the same century (431–404BC) they fought each other in a war which was eventually to ruin Athens.

▲ The picture on this *amphora* or vase shows a racing chariot with four horses at the Games. The Olympic Games were originally held as a religious ceremony in honour of Zeus. Women held their own games in honour of the goddess Hera. The Olympic Games were held every four years from 776BC to AD261. In 520BC the timetable for the events was as follows:

Day 1: sacrifices, oaths, checking of athletes.
Day 2: equestrian events, pentathlon.
Day 3: religious observations, boys' events.
Day 4: 'track' events, wrestling, boxing, race in armour.
Day 5: banquet, sacrifices.

◄ While marble statues often portrayed heroic figures of gods and goddesses, little clay figures portrayed the everyday life of ordinary people. This figure was made in 500BC and shows a woman grinding grain to make bread. Bread was the staple diet in most Greek towns, but eggs, vegetables, olives, grapes and figs were also grown and eaten. Meat was usually only eaten after a sacrifice.

Hadrian's Wall

BRITAIN

London
Londinium

Rhine

GERMANY

GAUL

Nîmes
Nemausus

Narbo

ITALY

Rome
Roma

Danube

BLACK SEA

Byzantium

Thessalonica

SPAIN

Carthage
Carthago

MEDITERRANEAN SEA

Antioch
Antiochia

AFRICA

SYRIA

EGYPT

Extent of Roman Empire AD 200

Roads

0   500 miles
0   500 kilometres

▼ This **aqueduct** was built across the Gard river in southern France in the time of the Emperor Augustus. The Romans were brilliant engineers and constructed roads, bridges, aqueducts and buildings all over their Empire, many of which are still standing. This aqueduct was used to take water to Nîmes where it was stored in a basin, with controlled outlets to both civic and private users.

▶ The ruins of the Colosseum, a huge **amphitheatre** in the centre of Rome. It was officially opened in AD80 and could hold 50,000 spectators. Both men and women came to watch the bloodthirsty fights to the death between gladiators (usually prisoners-of-war or condemned criminals), or between wild beasts. Beneath the floor of the amphitheatre were underground cages for the wild beasts, and a water system to flood the area for mock sea battles.

35

The Romans

The first civilization in Italy was that of the Etruscans who established small, independent city-states in the area which is now called Tuscany. We know little about the Etruscans, but they undoubtedly influenced their southern neighbours, the Romans, passing on, for example, their skill in building roads.

Rome itself was originally an Etruscan city but in 509BC the local aristocrats or 'patricians' expelled the Etruscan king and set up a **republic**. At first the patricians governed Rome: they elected two **consuls** from among themselves who were advised by the **Senate**. But gradually the ordinary people or 'plebeians' became more powerful and demanded a part in the government of Rome. After 367BC it became the custom for one consul to be a plebeian.

By 44BC the Romans ruled the whole Mediterranean world, either directly or by influence over native rulers. They linked together their huge Empire with a network of roads, and controlled it with a well-disciplined army. Trade flourished as the Roman way of life became established in many parts of the Empire: wine, olive oil, wool, linen and silk, spices, fine pottery and glass were all traded within the Empire.

The Roman Republic ended in a **civil war** in which one man, Octavian, gained supreme power. He was given the title Augustus and created himself Emperor.

▲ Part of Trajan's Column which tells the story of two of the wars fought by the Roman army under Trajan's command. The soldiers were well-trained and not only fought battles but also built bridges and fortresses; here they are building a camp, some soldiers are digging a double ditch, while others construct ramparts out of squared pieces of turf.

► A Roman family at dinner. The men recline on a couch to eat. Slaves stand by to wait on them.

▼ In his shop the Roman butcher wields a cleaver similar to those used today.

Religions of the Mediterranean Lands

Three important modern religions began close to the Mediterranean Sea: Judaism, Christianity and Islam. Unlike the eastern religions (*see page 25*) all three are based on a belief in one God.

Judaism

Judaism is the religion of Israel, and has been the religion of the Jews all over the world for more than 3000 years. Jews believe in one God whom they call *Yahweh* and he is the creator of all things.

The basis of Judaism is the Ten Commandments which, according to tradition, God gave to the Jewish leader Moses some time in the 1200sBC. The commandments and laws based on them rule every aspect of Jewish life. The history and laws of the Jews are contained in the Old Testament of the Bible.

▲ A mosaic of the seven-branched candlestick or Menorah. A golden Menorah stood in the tabernacle, the Jew's first holy temple.

Christianity

For centuries the Jews have believed that a Messiah (saviour) would be born to lead them. At the time that Jesus of Nazareth was born, around 4BC, the Jews were under Roman rule. Jesus's followers believed him to be the promised Messiah, the son of God, but other Jews accused him of blasphemy, and he was tried before the Roman governor of Judea, Pontius Pilate. Jesus was crucified, probably in about AD30, but his followers (disciples) reported having seen and talked to Jesus after his death. This resurrection formed the basis of the new religion that arose from the old traditions of Judaism: Christianity.

The life and teachings of Jesus are contained in the four Gospels of the New Testament of the Bible.

Islam

Islam is a much younger religion than either Judaism or Christianity. It was founded in the AD600s by the Prophet Muhammad. Muhammad was born in Mecca, an important trading centre in Arabia. At that time most Arabs believed in nature gods, spirits

▼ The Dome of the Rock, a Muslim mosque in Jerusalem. Jerusalem is a holy centre for Jews, Christians and Muslims.

and demons. One day Muhammad was sitting outside a cave when he heard a voice telling him to set down the words of God. His writings over the next 22 years were put together to form the Koran – the holy book of Islam.

The followers of Islam are called Muslims which means 'those who submit'. Muslims worship one god, Allah, and they have strict religious observances including regular prayer.

Peoples of the West and South

Although the civilizations of Europe and eastern Asia lay far apart, they were linked by traders even in ancient times. But there were two regions of the world which were completely cut off from the rest: the Americas and the Pacific. A third, Africa south of the Sahara, had comparatively few links.

The Americas

The first people to reach America probably walked across a land bridge where the Bering Strait now is (*see page 11*). The early Americans were hunters, fishers and food gatherers. They used stone tools and although metals such as gold, silver and copper were worked with hammers the secret of **smelting** was never discovered. Iron was not introduced into America until the European invasion in the AD1500s.

Farming began in an area called '**Mesoamerica**' by archaeologists, which includes central America and Mexico. Small villages grew up and people grew maize (corn), beans and pumpkins. Some of the earliest civilizations were also in this area: the Olmec culture with its centre at La Venta, the Teotihuacan culture, and the beginnings of the Maya culture which lasted until about AD1000.

► This little pottery figure of a crying baby is the work of the Olmec Amerindians who settled in communities on the coast of the Gulf of Mexico. Their centre was at La Venta. They invented a type of hieroglyphic writing and a numerical system.

▼ Huge stone heads, some of them 2.7 metres tall and weighing 15 tonnes, were carved by the Olmecs. They are thought to represent gods. The Olmec sculptors also carved small figures out of jade and similar hard stone.

▶ The hunters of the Arctic region used bone harpoons to catch seals and other sea mammals. The harpoons were carved with backward-projecting teeth so that they would not pull out of the prey once it was caught.

Early American Civilizations

Arctic Hunters

Coastal Fishers

Sub-Arctic Hunters

NORTH AMERICA

Hunters and Gatherers

Hopewell Indians

Woodland Farmers

PACIFIC OCEAN

MEXICO
Teotihuacan
Olmec Culture
La Venta
Maya Culture
CENTRAL AMERICA

ATLANTIC OCEAN

Farming tribes

Chavin

SOUTH AMERICA

Hunters

▲ The great Serpent Mound in Ohio built by the Hopewell Indians in about AD200. The Hopewell people were hunters who also cultivated maize. They buried their dead in huge mounds.

▼ This bowl, carved in animal form, is the work of the Chavin Amerindians who developed the first civilization in Peru from about 1000 to 300BC. They built small settlements around the ceremonial pyramids where they paid tribute to their priests and gods.

0   800 kilometres
0   500 miles

African Empires

Up until the end of the last ice age the area which we now call the Sahara was not desert but wet grassland. In this fertile region the early African peoples cultivated wheat and barley and herded cattle. But after about 2500BC the climate slowly became warmer and the Sahara began to dry out. Some of the farmers moved gradually southwards to the **tropical** regions of the interior. Here, after about 2000BC, sorghum, millet and yams were cultivated: elsewhere, in places where the jungle was too thick for crop-growing, local economies were sometimes based on fishing.

The earliest African civilization south of the great Egyptian Empire (*see pages 16–18*) was the kingdom of Kush, which flourished on the banks of the Nile from about 500BC to AD350. Its capital, Meroë, was an important centre for iron-working from about 500BC, and this skill quickly spread south. People could now make iron tools and weapons, cultivation was easier and crops improved.

The Bantu peoples

South of the rain forests of the Congo Basin the earliest inhabitants were hunters; the San and the Khoi-khoi peoples. But gradually a new group of people migrated from their homeland in the north and west and developed their own cultures. They had one linking feature which was that their languages all came from the same root; **Bantu**.

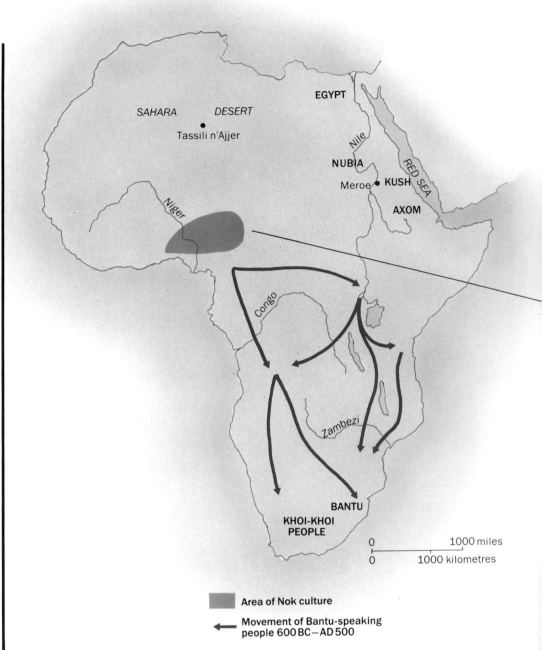

Area of Nok culture

Movement of Bantu-speaking people 600 BC – AD 500

▼ Methods of iron smelting were developed in Africa after about 500BC. In this picture the furnace is built of compacted earth and bellows are used to reach the high temperatures necessary to turn the iron ore into metal. The metal produced was used to make strong tools and weapons.

40,000BC–AD456

▼ One of the fine terracotta heads found near the village of Nok, in northern Nigeria. This type of sculpture flourished in the area from about 400BC to AD200.

▲ Three important crops which were cultivated by early farmers south of the Sahara.
1. Sorghum, an important early crop.
2. Millet, faster-growing than sorghum and able to withstand a drier climate.
3. Yam, a nutritious tuber.

▼ Rock paintings and relief carvings are found all over Africa. This lively cattle-herding scene comes from the Tassili-n-Ajjer Mountains in the Sahara. The first **pastoralists** in the Sahara region protected goats and sheep; later many different breeds of cattle were kept.

Australia and Oceania

The first people migrated to Australia between 70,000 and 50,000 years ago. At that time the sea levels were lower than they are today, so that Australia, New Guinea and Tasmania were all joined by huge land bridges, forming a land mass called 'Greater Australia'. The first Australians, ancestors of the Aborigines, had to sail across the sea from south-east Asia to reach the nearest point of Greater Australia.

Around 6000 years ago the sea rose to its present level, and the Aboriginal people began to move into the interior and exploit the natural resources found there. The Aborigines were fishers, hunters and gatherers: they never developed a system of agriculture or cattle-rearing. They developed their own culture until the arrival of the Europeans in the AD1700s.

The smaller Pacific Islands which make up Oceania, spread out over the vast Pacific Ocean, were colonized much later. The first people sailed from the Moluccas region of Indonesia in about 2000BC. These people were able to build large canoes that could survive long voyages, and transport not only them but their supplies, animals and some of the plants they grew. They sailed first to the islands of Melanesia, then in about 1300BC they reached Fiji, Samoa and Tonga. The farthest islands of Oceania, and New Zealand, were not settled until at least AD800.

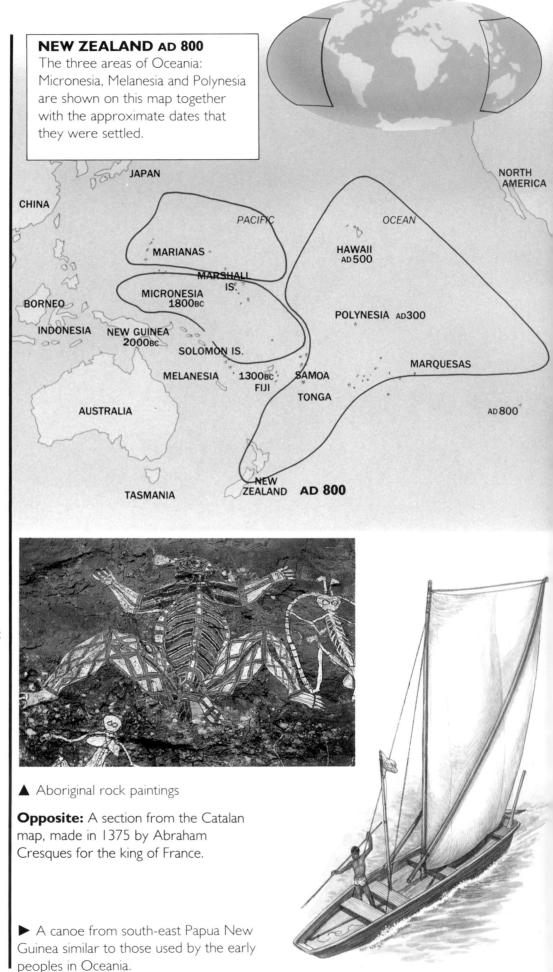

NEW ZEALAND AD 800
The three areas of Oceania: Micronesia, Melanesia and Polynesia are shown on this map together with the approximate dates that they were settled.

▲ Aboriginal rock paintings

Opposite: A section from the Catalan map, made in 1375 by Abraham Cresques for the king of France.

► A canoe from south-east Papua New Guinea similar to those used by the early peoples in Oceania.

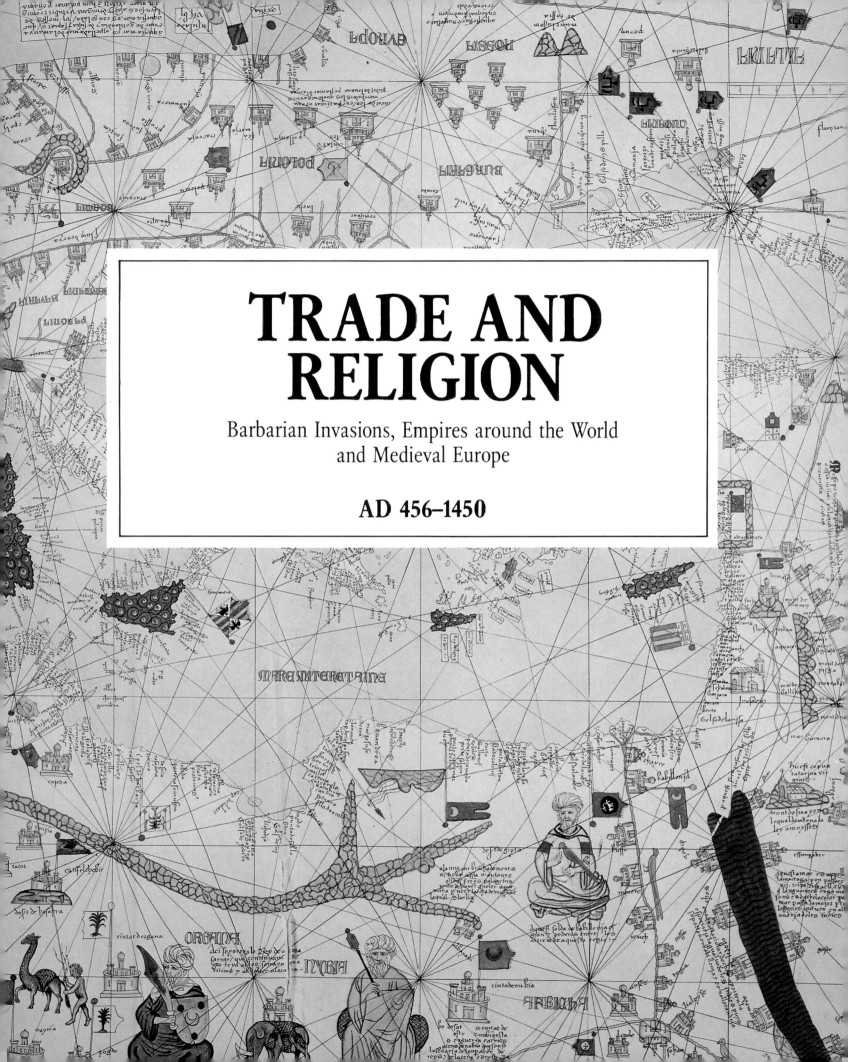

TRADE AND RELIGION

Barbarian Invasions, Empires around the World
and Medieval Europe

AD 456–1450

The World in 450 and After

The world in 450

About 2000 years ago, most people in the world lived within four great **empires**. The Roman Empire was the most powerful, and controlled Europe and north Africa. To the east, the Han **Dynasty** (family) governed much of what is now modern China. Between them lay the rich Sassanian Empire in the Middle East, and the great Gupta Empire of India.

These powerful empires were secure and peaceful, with strong governments and wealthy **economies**. **Trade** linked them all together. Land travel was slow, however, and many goods were transported on boats, which crossed both the Indian Ocean and the Mediterranean Sea. These trading contacts brought the peoples of the four empires together and helped the spread of religious and other ideas.

These links did not stretch across either the Pacific or Atlantic Oceans. As a result, the peoples of Australia and America developed **cultures** of their own. Much of Africa, too, developed independently of the rest of the world.

By 450 the great empires of the world were under threat from various warlike **tribes** of **nomads** in northern Europe and parts of Asia. Within a few years these tribes were to disrupt the settled empires.

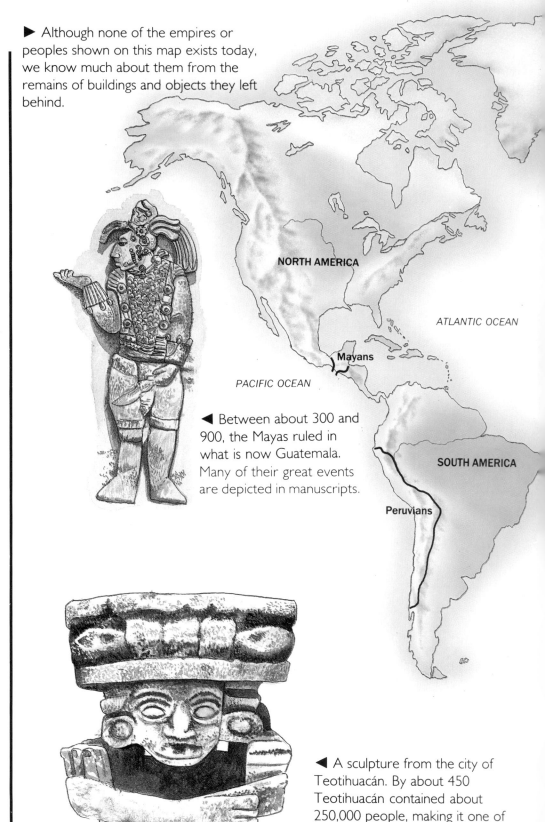

► Although none of the empires or peoples shown on this map exists today, we know much about them from the remains of buildings and objects they left behind.

◄ Between about 300 and 900, the Mayas ruled in what is now Guatemala. Many of their great events are depicted in manuscripts.

◄ A sculpture from the city of Teotihuacán. By about 450 Teotihuacán contained about 250,000 people, making it one of the biggest cities in the world at that time.

44

► The Romans were skilled builders and constructed houses and public buildings in all parts of their Empire. The remains of this steam bath are in Ephesus, in Turkey.

EUROPE

ASIA

Rome
Roman Empire
Mediterranean Sea
Alexandria

Sassanian
Empire

CHINA
Han Dynasty

Gupta
Empire

INDIA

PACIFIC OCEAN

Red Sea

Axum

AFRICA

INDIAN OCEAN

AUSTRALIA

◄ The Sassanian Empire in the Middle East reached its greatest extent in 579. Its peoples were skilled at metal work as can be seen from this silver dish, showing a Sassanian king out hunting.

► The kingdom of Axum controlled the Red Sea trade route leading to Alexandria, the centre of east–west trade. Its people erected giant obelisks over 30 metres high, as a mark of their country's importance.

45

The collapse of empires

Ever since 200BC, the four empires in Europe and Asia had come under threat from heavily armed nomadic tribes. The Romans called them **Barbarians**, for they were not educated and were not Christians. Nor did they live in settled towns but in tents on the vast **steppes** of central Asia. They travelled thousands of miles in search of grazing land, and when the pasture land was exhausted, or if they were attacked by rival tribes, they moved in search of new land, threatening the settled empires to the south and west.

At first, both the Romans and Chinese kept the nomads out, building strong defences such as Hadrian's Wall in Britain and the Great Wall in China. These defences were expensive and the high **taxes** imposed to pay for them caused rebellions which weakened both the Chinese and Roman Empires.

China was the first empire to fall. In 220, the Hsiungnu peoples of central Asia attacked China and ended Han rule in the country. The Huns, part of the Hsiungnu tribe, killed the Persian Emperor in 484, and by 535 had destroyed the Gupta Empire in India.

But it was the Roman Empire that suffered the most. Tribes had attacked the Roman Empire as early as 167, but after 370 the attacks were more serious and Rome was overrun. In 476, the last Roman Emperor was overthrown and the Empire was replaced by small tribal kingdoms.

▲ Because little written evidence exists about the fall of the Roman Empire, we have to learn about it from craftworks, buildings and carvings. This carving is on the side of a tomb dating from around 200, and shows Roman soldiers fighting German invaders.

▶ The peoples who invaded the Roman Empire were skilled craft workers. This elaborate helmet of iron, bronze and silver was made by the Saxon invaders of Britain in about 625.

▼ Many of the tribes that invaded the Roman Empire adopted its official religion of Christianity. This gold helmet plaque shows an Ostrogoth ruler surrounded by angels.

▲ From about 167 a number of warring tribes attacked the long land frontier of the Roman Empire in central Europe. At first they were kept out of the Empire. But when the Huns arrived in eastern Europe from central Asia around 370, many tribes started pouring over the frontier. The Visigoths sacked Rome in 410 and moved on to settle in southern Spain, while the Vandals moved into Spain by 409 and north Africa in 429. In the north, the Franks settled in what is now France, while the Angles, Saxons and Jutes invaded Britain.

▶ The Vandals invaded north Africa and set up their capital at Carthage. They took over the existing city and lived in the Roman houses, adopting Roman clothes and ways of life. This **mosaic**, made in about 500, shows a Vandal warrior leaving his villa as if he were a Roman citizen, not a conqueror.

The Byzantine Empire

In 284, Diocletian became Roman Emperor. He decided that the huge Empire could only be ruled effectively by splitting it into two parts, east and west. In 330 his successor, Constantine, rebuilt the old Greek port of Byzantium, at the entrance to the Black Sea, and renamed it Constantinople. This city became the capital of the eastern half of the Empire. When the western half collapsed during the next century, Constantinople became the capital of the new Byzantine Empire.

At first, this Empire only controlled a small area around the eastern Mediterranean, but during the reign of Justinian (527–65), it started to recover much of the territory of the old Roman Empire. North Africa, Italy and southern Spain were all reconquered.

The Byzantine Empire was wealthy, producing gold, silk, grain, olives and wine, and these were traded for spices, precious stones, furs and ivory with countries as far afield as China and India. The Empire was a centre of learning, combining the knowledge of the Ancient Greeks with the newer teachings of the Christian Church.

However, by 750, the last invaders from the east – Bulgars, Slavs and Lombards – reduced the Empire to a small area of what is now Greece and Turkey, and it never regained its strength. Yet it lasted until 1453, when the city of Constantinople was finally captured by the Turks.

▲ The Byzantine Empire was ruled from its capital city of Constantinople, known today as Istanbul. At first the Empire lay around the Aegean Sea. It reached its greatest extent under Justinian, when it spread across the Mediterranean to Spain. However, it was always under threat from its warlike neighbours.

▼ This old map of Constantinople shows fortifications and many fine buildings. The city was an important trading centre and commanded both the sea route between the Mediterranean and the Black Sea, and the land route between Europe and Asia and on to China.

▼ Many churches and public buildings in the Byzantine Empire were decorated with elaborate mosaics. These were made of thousands of coloured glass cubes set in plaster. Some of the cubes were covered with gold or silver dust to make them glisten in the light.

▼ The Byzantine Empire was often under attack both from sea and from land. The secret weapon of the Byzantine navy was 'Greek Fire', a chemical mixture which burst into flames when it touched water.

▲ Under Justinian and Empress Theodora, the Byzantine Empire was a centre for the arts and learning. This mosaic of Justinian is in the church of San Vitale in Ravenna, for a time the capital of the Byzantine Empire in Italy.

The decimal system

Sometime after 400 the Guptas of India developed a new method of counting, which was based on multiples of 10. They used the symbol 0 to represent zero and the symbol . to separate whole numbers from fractions. From this came the decimal system that we use today. The Guptas also designed a simple way of writing numbers down. We call these numbers 'Arabic' numerals, because, like the decimal system, they came to us from the Arabs whose traders learned them in India and brought them to Europe sometime after 1300.

The Religious World

All of the major religions have begun in Asia. Three of them – Judaism, Christianity and **Islam** – started in the Middle East and their followers regard Jerusalem as a holy city. These religions have spread across the world as **missionaries**, traders and other people travelled along the trade routes.

Early Christianity

Christianity began in the Roman province of Judaea, in what is now Israel. Originally it was part of the Jewish religion. But in about AD30, when its founder, Jesus Christ, was put to death by the Romans, his followers became known as Christians and founded a new religion based on the teachings of Christ.

The early Christians travelled throughout the Roman Empire preaching the message of Christ. At first the Romans persecuted them. But in 312 the Roman Emperor Constantine legalized Christianity and it became the official religion of the Roman Empire in 392. Christianity grew in strength because it offered hope to its followers in the troubled times. Many of the invading tribes also adopted Christianity, but it spread slowly, and in some places, such as the British Isles, the early Christians had to struggle to keep the religion alive.

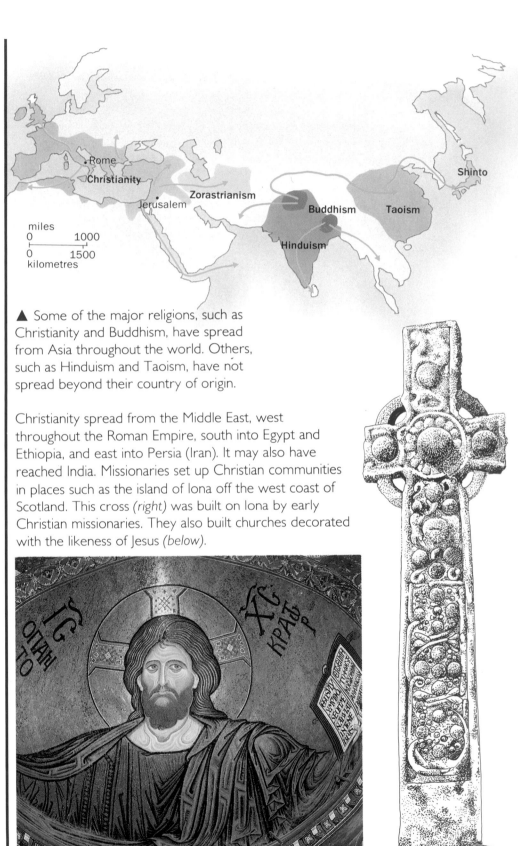

▲ Some of the major religions, such as Christianity and Buddhism, have spread from Asia throughout the world. Others, such as Hinduism and Taoism, have not spread beyond their country of origin.

Christianity spread from the Middle East, west throughout the Roman Empire, south into Egypt and Ethiopia, and east into Persia (Iran). It may also have reached India. Missionaries set up Christian communities in places such as the island of Iona off the west coast of Scotland. This cross (right) was built on Iona by early Christian missionaries. They also built churches decorated with the likeness of Jesus (below).

▼ Some early Christians built religious communities called monasteries where they could worship God away from the distractions of daily life. The Christians who lived in them were called monks. In a monastery, there was an abbey or church in which to worship, buildings for living and working, and gardens for growing the food. This detailed plan (left) shows us how early monasteries were laid out and how they would have looked (below), although this particular monastery was never built.

▶ Monasteries were important centres of learning because monks were almost the only people who could read and write. Monks drew up official documents, kept records and wrote letters. They also copied books (right), which was the only way a book could be reproduced, for printing presses were unknown in Europe until 1453. Copying was done by hand and could take many years. Some monks were skilled illustrators, as can be seen from this detail (far right) in the beautiful Book of Kells, a religious manuscript which was produced on the Scottish island of Iona in about 800.

51

The rise of Islam

In the 600s, a new religion began in Arabia. It was called Islam, which means 'Submission to the will of Allah (God)'. Within 100 years, more than half the total population of Europe and Asia was Muslim (the name given to followers of Islam).

Islam was founded by a prophet called Muhammad. He came from the Arabian city of Mecca and in about 610 began to write the Koran, the holy book of Islam. The new religion threatened the old gods worshipped in Mecca, so in 622 Muhammad and his followers were forced to flee to the nearby town of Medina.

From Medina, Muhammad and his followers organized the first Muslim **state** and built the first mosque. Although Arabia was a wealthy region, most of the population was very poor. Many of these poor people were attracted to Islam because its teachings offered them a fairer society.

In 630 Muhammad attacked and captured Mecca. Under his rule, as **Caliph**, Mecca became the capital of an Islamic empire that controlled most of the Arabian peninsula. After Muhammad's death in 632, Muslim armies spread the Islamic religion eastwards to India and westwards across north Africa and into Spain. The Byzantine Empire was seriously weakened and lost all its lands in Africa. But the Muslims were defeated by the Franks in France at the battle of Poitiers in 732 and their empire extended no farther.

▲ The Kaaba in Mecca houses a sacred black stone and is the centre of the Islamic world. At certain times during the day, every Muslim in the world faces towards it to pray. **Pilgrims** to Mecca walk around it seven times in homage.

◀ The Koran is the holy book of Islam. Muslims believe that it is the word of God as told to his prophet Muhammad. The Koran contains religious beliefs as well as social and political instructions.

▼ Islam began in Arabia but quickly spread throughout the Middle East and north Africa by 750 (shaded area on map below). Although united by one faith, the Islamic world soon broke up into separate countries.

Poitiers

SPAIN

Constantinople

Damascus
Jerusalem
Baghdad

Cairo

EGYPT
ARABIA
INDIA

Medina

Mecca

—— Byzantine Empire

miles
0   500

0   800
kilometres

Arab Science and Learning

In 762, Al-Mansur, the leader of the Islamic world, built a new capital city at Baghdad in what is now Iraq. He made it a centre of learning and culture. There was an observatory to study the stars and a 'House of Learning' in which scholars studied mathematics and translated the writings of the Ancient Greeks into Arabic. Christian and Jewish scholars were welcomed because Islam was tolerant of other religions. Cairo, in Egypt, was also a centre of learning, and in 971, the world's first university was opened there. The arts flourished throughout the Islamic world, particularly calligraphy or writing. This was because it was forbidden to draw or paint human figures in religious pictures.

▲ Arab astronomers, like the Ancient Greeks, showed the constellations of the stars as human figures. The constellation shown here is Cepheus.

▲ Water was scarce in the hot, dry climate of the Islamic world. Arab engineers were skilled in methods of raising water from the ground and piping it into their homes.

▲ In 1154, Arab map-makers drew this map of the world. It shows that they were familiar with the basic outlines of Asia, north Africa and Europe. But like the Europeans at this time, they did not know that Australia or America existed.

▲ Arab medicine was very advanced. Islamic pharmacists or chemists were skilled in making up suitable drugs for treating illnesses.

53

The Buddhist world

Buddhism, one of the world's greatest religions, began as an offshoot of Hinduism, an Indian religion that dates back to 1500BC and is still widely practised today. The Hindus divided people up into social classes called **castes**. They believed that a person was born into one particular caste and could not leave it during his or her lifetime. But many people disliked this strict system because it meant that nothing could be changed and that suffering and poverty were allowed to continue.

In about 525BC, an Indian prince called Gautama Siddhartha, who had left his rich family to travel and study, began to preach another message. He said that it was possible to overcome suffering and reach a state of total peace, which he called 'Nirvana'.

By the time of his death in 483BC, Gautama had become known as the Buddha or 'the Enlightened One' and his teachings spread throughout India. In about 257BC, the Indian ruler Asoka became a Buddhist, and Buddhism became a major force throughout southern Asia. Missionaries spread the religion north to Afghanistan, Tibet, China and Japan, where it became the official religion in 594. They also spread Buddhism south to Burma and the rest of Indochina. Buddhism gained strength from the upheavals caused by the nomadic invasions. In 624 Buddhism became the official religion of China.

▲ Missionaries spread the Buddhist religion from India north to Afghanistan, Tibet, China, and Japan and south to Burma and Indochina, often following trade routes.

▼ The Buddhist temple of Borobudur in Java was built about 800. It has ten levels. Each level represents the different stages of a person's life from ignorance to Nirvana, the ultimate Buddhist aim.

► When the Chinese Princess Yung T'ai was only 17, she was forced to commit suicide for criticizing her grandmother, the Chinese Empress Wu (690–713). Yung T'ai's tomb is decorated with portraits of court ladies accompanied by servants waiting on the princess.

▼ During the time of the Sui Dynasty in China (581–618), more than 100,000 statues of Buddha were built, some out of solid rock, and nearly 4000 temples were constructed.

Footbinding
In Chinese culture, small feet were considered a sign of beauty. The daughters of the wealthy classes had their feet bound tightly with silk when they were very young. As they grew up, their feet stayed so small that the women could not walk without considerable pain. Footbinding continued in China almost to the present day.

55

Empires and Invasions

Charlemagne and the Holy Roman Empire

On Christmas Day in 800, the Pope crowned a new Roman Emperor, Charles the Great, or Charlemagne as he is better known.

Charlemagne was a Frank, one of the peoples who had invaded the Roman Empire and settled in what is now central France. The leader of the Franks, Clovis, was a Christian and had founded the Merovingian Dynasty of kings. But following Frankish tradition, the kingdom had been divided between the various royal sons. This weakened it so much that power fell into the hands of leading officials. In 751, one of the officials, Pepin, deposed the Merovingians and formed the Carolingian Dynasty. In 768, Pepin's two sons, Carloman and Charlemagne inherited the kingdom, and in 771, when his brother died, Charlemagne took full control.

Charlemagne soon conquered the rest of France and extended his kingdom into what is now Germany, Italy and The Netherlands. He forcibly converted to Christianity the Saxons and Avars who lived in central Europe. By the time of his death in 814, the Franks were the most powerful force in western Europe.

Frankish Empire in 771

land conquered by Charlemagne

— divisions of Charlemagne's empire in 870

The Holy Roman Empire

When Charlemagne was crowned in 800, he founded an empire that later became known as the Holy Roman Empire. This Empire lasted 1000 years until 1806 when it was abolished by the French Emperor, Napoleon Bonaparte. It was revived briefly between 1871 and 1918 when Germany was united as one country for the first time. Between 1933 and 1945, the German dictator, Adolf Hitler, attempted to build a Third Reich (Empire) to last a further 1000 years, but he was defeated.

▲ Charlemagne's empire stretched from northern Spain across Europe to Germany and Italy. When it was divided between his three grandsons in 843, and again in 870, the boundaries of present-day France, Italy and Germany became recognizable for the first time.

▼ The scholars who came to Charlemagne's court at Aachen in Germany developed a new style of handwriting in which to write their books. This was Carolingian **minuscule**, used by the first printers 600 years later when they designed a type in which to print the first books.

BEATISSIMO PAPAE DAMASO
bIERONIMUS

Trade and Transport

Before cars, trains and aeroplanes were invented, most people never left the town or village in which they were born. People worked within walking distance of their houses and no one took holidays away from home. The only people who travelled were soldiers, traders, government officials and pilgrims going to visit religious sites. They walked or rode on horseback along rough roads and their journeys were slow and often dangerous. On land, robbers attacked foot travellers, while pirate raids were common at sea. But despite these problems, many travellers covered great distances and the main roads were often very busy.

◀ Travelling could be hazardous. Here a traveller surrenders his money to a highwayman.

▲ Trade was carried across the Indian Ocean by ships called *dhows*. These simple but safe ships had lots of room for both passengers and cargo.

◀ Merchants, craftworkers and buyers gathered at the fairs which were held in large towns all over Europe. This fair at Lendit in France started off as a religious festival.

▲ The **Silk Road** was the main land route between China and Europe. It was 4000 kilometres long and the best way to travel along it was by camel.

Viking invasions

Peace in western Europe did not last long. After 900, Muslim Arabs from north Africa conquered Italy and crossed the Pyrenees to threaten France. The Magyars, another group of Asian nomads, raided Germany and Italy.

But the most powerful threat came from the Viking peoples of Scandinavia – Sweden, Norway and Denmark. They left their homes in search of wealth and better farmland. They were skilled seafarers, and sailed vast distances in their open longboats.

In 793 the Vikings raided Britain and soon occupied the northern half of the country. They established colonies in Ireland, and by 911 had settled in northern France, where they became known as Normans. They also travelled to Iceland and Greenland, and, in 1003, reached Vinland (probably Newfoundland, Canada), almost 500 years before the Genoese explorer Columbus claimed to have discovered the same continent. A group of Vikings from Sweden, known as the Rus, set up trading posts at Novgorod and Kiev, giving their name – Russia – to the country they colonized.

Stories of the exploits of the Vikings were written by the people they attacked. These accounts naturally describe the Vikings as savage raiders, but they were also skilled craft-workers. The colonies they founded grew rich on trade, and the Vikings soon settled peacefully with the peoples they had once fought.

▶ Usually the Vikings met little resistance from the peoples whose lands they invaded, but they did meet stiff opposition from the people of Wessex, in the south of England. In 878, Wessex troops, led by their king, Alfred, beat the Vikings and forced them back to the north of the country. This gold and enamel jewel depicts Alfred, and may have been owned by him, for the writing round the edge states that 'Alfred had me made'.

▼ Because the Viking buildings were made of wood rather than stone, little remains for us to see today. But some objects have survived and give us an idea of how the Vikings lived, what they wore and the crafts they practised.

spoon

pendant

brooches

silver arm-ring

leather ankle-boot on a skate made of bone

bowl and spoon

The Vikings travelled thousands of miles. Vikings from Sweden dragged their ships overland before sailing down the Russian rivers to the Black Sea and Constantinople. Vikings from Norway and Denmark sailed across the North Sea to France, Britain and Ireland. Some also crossed the Atlantic to discover Iceland, Greenland and a place they called Vinland. They may even have sailed as far south as Florida.

▲ The Vikings excelled at metalwork. This die, used to stamp an identifying picture on a metal sheet, shows two legendary warriors about to attack a ferocious beast.

▼ The main reason for the success of the Vikings was the speed and seaworthiness of their longboats. The Vikings believed that the spirits of past leaders lived in the boats. For this reason, they buried their leaders with their ships when they died. This longboat was made for a queen and was found preserved in the mud at Oseberg in Norway

▲ The Vikings could not read or write, so **sagas** or legends about their gods and heroes were learned by heart and handed down from parent to child by word of mouth. This wood carving shows the legendary hero Sigurd killing Fafnir the dragon.

59

Norman invaders

In 1066 Edward the Confessor, the King of England, died. He had no children to succeed him and so three people claimed the English throne. They were Harold, Earl of Wessex (who was Edward's choice as his successor), the King of Norway and William, Duke of Normandy, who was Edward's cousin. Harold was crowned king but immediately the other two **claimants** prepared to attack Harold and seize the throne.

The King of Norway was the first to attack. He sailed over the North Sea with an army and landed in the north of England. There he was quickly defeated by Harold and killed in battle. But then William, Duke of Normandy, landed with a large army on the south coast of England. William was a descendant of the Viking invaders of northern France who had settled there in 911 and had become known as Normans. William claimed that Harold had once promised to support his claim to be king. Harold headed south to fight William's army but was defeated by them at a battle outside Hastings. William 'the Conqueror' then marched to London and was crowned King of England on Christmas Day, 1066.

William set about controlling his new kingdom by building fortified castles and giving lands and titles to his Norman followers. He soon overcame English opposition to his rule and ruled securely until the time of his death in 1087.

▲ The Bayeux Tapestry tells the story of the Norman invasion of England. The tapestry is more than 70 metres long and was made soon after the invasion in 1066. This section shows the Norman fleet crossing the English Channel.

◀ The kings of England were also dukes of Normandy and acquired further land in France through marriage. By 1154, they ruled over a greater area of France than the French king.

◀ In 1086 William the Conqueror ordered that a list be made of all the landowners in his new kingdom. The list took a year to compile and the results were recorded in the Domesday Book (in fact, two volumes). Domesday means 'Doomsday', or 'day of judgement'.

Castles

▲ Laying siege to a castle

The lord or **baron** of an area built a castle to defend the surrounding countryside, administer his lands and to provide a safe home for his family to live in. A castle was therefore a military barracks, an office and a house. The castle was protected from attack by a moat full of water which could only be crossed by a drawbridge. This would be raised in times of danger. A high wall surrounded an inner courtyard where there were stables for horses and living quarters for soldiers. Local people could bring their animals into the courtyard if they were attacked. At the centre of the castle stood the keep, a fortified house in which the lord and lady of the castle lived.

Keep

Living quarters

Great Hall

Chapel

Guardroom for soldiers

Stables for horses

Dungeon and storerooms

Courtyard

Outer walls and battlements

Portcullis

Turret

Drawbridge

Moat

▲ Castles were designed to be safe from attack, with high walls and a deep moat to prevent the enemy from getting in. Many castles were built on tops of hills or by the sides of rivers, which made it difficult for enemies to get close to them.

61

The Crusades

From about 200, Christian pilgrims from Europe travelled to Jerusalem and other parts of the Holy Land to worship in the places where Christianity had begun. But from 638, the Holy Land was controlled by Muslim Arabs. At first the Muslims did not interfere with the pilgrims, but in 1071 the Turks conquered the area. They attacked and killed the pilgrims and prevented Christians from worshipping in Jerusalem.

In 1095, Pope Urban the Second called on all Christians to go on **crusades** to the Holy Land to fight a holy war against the Turks. Within a year, a large army from all over Europe had gathered at Constantinople. When the Crusaders reached the Holy Land in 1099, they captured Jerusalem and set up several Christian kingdoms in the area.

Nine further Crusades were organized between 1147 and 1271 but none was as successful as the first. After Jerusalem was recaptured by the Muslims in 1187, a Children's Crusade attempted to recapture it in 1212. But the children were not armed and most were sold into slavery before they even reached the Holy Land. In 1291 the Christians were finally thrown out of the Holy Land.

The Crusades failed for many reasons. The Crusaders were often poorly equipped, and they frequently quarrelled among themselves. Many had gone to the Holy Land to make themselves rich, not to defend their religion.

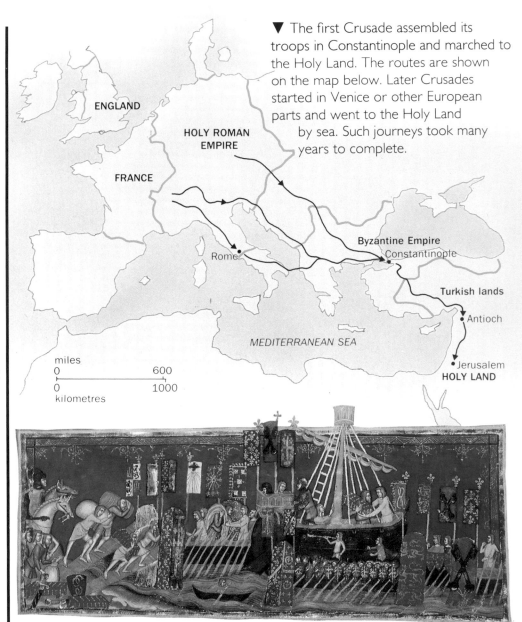

▼ The first Crusade assembled its troops in Constantinople and marched to the Holy Land. The routes are shown on the map below. Later Crusades started in Venice or other European parts and went to the Holy Land by sea. Such journeys took many years to complete.

ENGLAND

HOLY ROMAN EMPIRE

FRANCE

Rome

Byzantine Empire
Constantinople

Turkish lands

Antioch

MEDITERRANEAN SEA

Jerusalem
HOLY LAND

miles
0   600
0   1000
kilometres

▲ Embarking stores and provisions for a Crusade.

◄ Krak des Chevaliers (Castle of the Knights) in Syria was one of the strongest of the Crusader castles, built to guard the routes from the East to the Mediterranean coast.

◄ A knight would consider the rescue of a damsel in distress as a great honour. The highest duty of a knight was to protect vulnerable people.

▼ As part of the tournament splendid banquets were held for the knights, lords and ladies. After the meal the guests performed dances.

At the time of the Crusades, warfare was considered a worthwhile occupation and young men spent many hours practising the skills they would need on the battlefield. Mock battles, or **tournaments**, were held where sword fights and other contests of skill took place. Strict rules regulated these contests because they could be dangerous. The young knights were carefully dressed in armour to prevent them getting hurt (*above*) and they fought on behalf of a woman who made sure that the contest was fair. The most important contest was the joust (*right*), where two mounted horsemen charged each other and tried to unseat their opponent with a lance.

63

Empires beyond Europe

The Mayas of America

The peoples of the American continent remained isolated, apart from the Vikings' brief visit to north America in 1003. Many ideas and inventions that were developed in Europe and Asia, such as the wheel and the plough, remained unknown in America. Instead, the Americans developed their own civilizations without any outside contact.

Between 300 and 900, the Mayas of Central America built a flourishing empire, with huge cities dominated by massive temples where they worshipped their gods. They were skilled astronomers and mathematicians and were the only American people who could read or write. Another major civilization was the city-state of Teotihuacán, where 250,000 people lived. The city covered 13 square kilometres and was one of the largest in the world, even bigger than Rome, then the largest city in Europe. Both the Mayan Empire and the city of Teotihuacán started to decline in about 750. In 900 the Mayas were replaced as the greatest power in America by the Toltecs. In 1200 the Toltecs themselves were replaced by the Aztecs.

The other great civilizations in America were in the Andes Mountains to the south. There, up to 100,000 people lived in

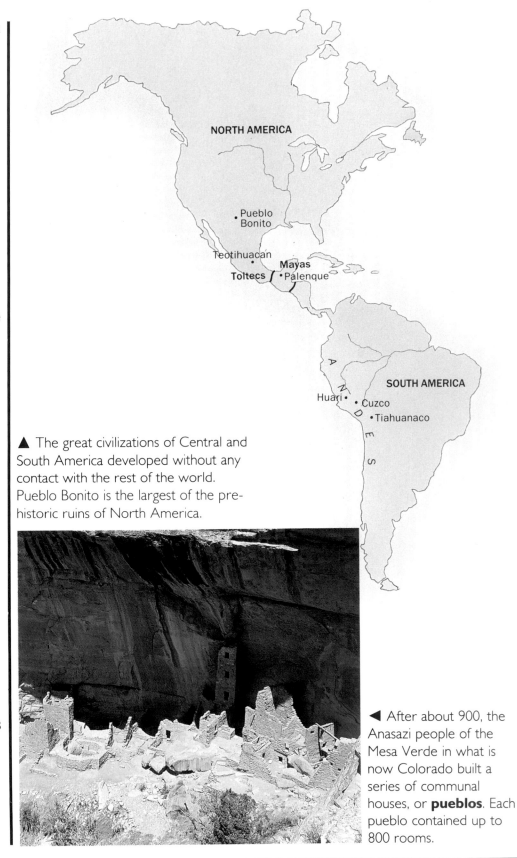

▲ The great civilizations of Central and South America developed without any contact with the rest of the world. Pueblo Bonito is the largest of the pre-historic ruins of North America.

◄ After about 900, the Anasazi people of the Mesa Verde in what is now Colorado built a series of communal houses, or **pueblos**. Each pueblo contained up to 800 rooms.

450–1450

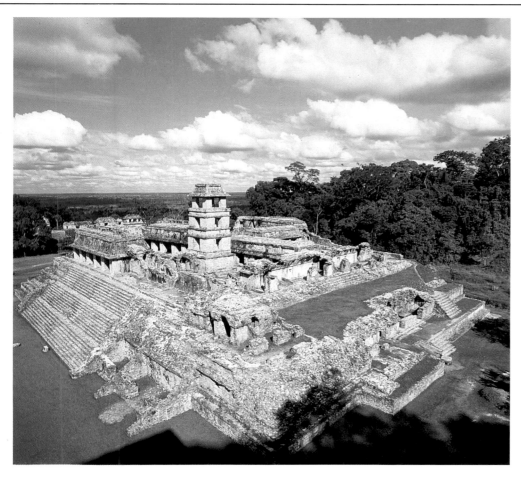

◀ At the centre of their cities the Mayas built pyramid-shaped temples surrounded by large palaces. This one is at Palenque in Mexico. Thousands of workers were required to construct these buildings. Many thousands more worked in the fields nearby to provide food for the workers.

▼ The Toltecs lived in central Mexico and governed a large empire which traded throughout the region. In their capital, Tula, they built many temples, guarded by stone statues of warriors.

The Mayan language
The Mayas wrote in a picture alphabet that no one else understood *(below)*. Only three of their documents survived the Spanish invasion in the 1530s. In the 1880s a scholar translated one document and began to decipher the Mayan language. However, many Mayan symbols are still not understood today.

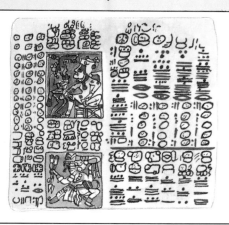

▲ The symbol of the cat appears throughout Central and South America on sculptures, carvings, pottery, and, as here. on a tapestry. In Peru, the city of Cuzco is thought to have been arranged in the shape of a puma.

the cities of Tiahuanaco and Huari. Like the cities to the north, both Tiahuanaco and Huari were full of temples decorated with intricate carvings and both were the capitals of powerful empires.

Trade in Africa

South of the Sahara a number of countries developed and grew rich on trade and **commerce**. The kingdom of Ghana controlled the trade that flowed along the Niger River and sold spices and gold to the Arabs who crossed the Sahara. The Arabs brought their Muslim religion with them and gradually they converted the people of Ghana and the neighbouring areas to Islam. By 1300 the great trading cities of Jenne and Timbuctu were centres of Islamic learning and attracted scholars from all over west and north Africa.

On the east coast of Africa, the ports of Kilwa and Gedi exported ivory, spices and gold to Arabia, India and China, and imported carpets, ceramics and horses in return. In 1071, **ambassadors** were sent to China to establish trading contacts and fleets of Chinese **junks** visited the ports in 1418 and 1422, keen to buy the goods that were on sale.

Farther south, Great Zimbabwe was a wealthy state that grew rich on gold mining and cattle herding. The gold was taken overland to Sofala, where it was traded for beads, porcelain and other luxuries with the Arab traders who sailed south down the east coast of Africa.

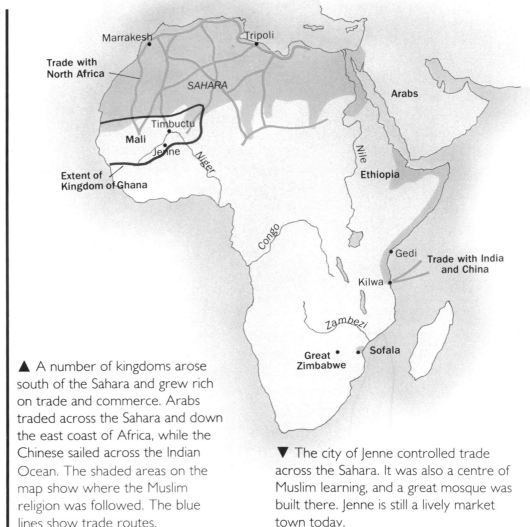

▲ A number of kingdoms arose south of the Sahara and grew rich on trade and commerce. Arabs traded across the Sahara and down the east coast of Africa, while the Chinese sailed across the Indian Ocean. The shaded areas on the map show where the Muslim religion was followed. The blue lines show trade routes.

▼ The city of Jenne controlled trade across the Sahara. It was also a centre of Muslim learning, and a great mosque was built there. Jenne is still a lively market town today.

▲ The cities of east Africa, such as Kilwa, conducted trade across the Indian Ocean with India and China. In 1414, east African ambassadors visited the Chinese Emperor with gifts, including a giraffe.

▼ Great Zimbabwe was the capital of a major trading empire that dominated southern Africa in the 1300s. The gold, iron and copper mined in the region were much in demand throughout Africa. Many of the ruins of the huge defensive walls and towers of the city can be seen today.

▲ The only practical way for Arab traders to cross the vast and inhospitable Sahara was by camel. Groups of traders travelled together for safety. These groups were called *caravans*. While some camels were ridden, many others were used to carry the traders' heavy loads. Although jeeps and lorries have now largely replaced them, camels are still used today for transport in the desert.

▲ Ethiopia was the only Christian country in Africa. In 1200, the kings of Ethiopia constructed 11 churches out of solid rock. The church of St George at Lalibela is shaped like a cross and, in common with the other churches, is still in use today.

67

Mongol invasions

The Mongols were tribes of nomads from the steppes or plains of central Asia. The different tribes often quarrelled among themselves, and it was not until 1206 that one of their leaders, Temujin, was proclaimed supreme ruler. He took the name Genghis Khan, which means 'Prince of all that lies between the Oceans', and his forces soon began to conquer the surrounding countries.

In 1211 the Mongols invaded China and captured its capital Beijing (Peking) in 1215. They then turned west and by 1223 had conquered central Asia. Genghis Khan died in 1227 but his son Ogedei continued the conquests in Russia, Hungary and on the shores of the Adriatic Sea. The Mongols had an army of 150,000 men and there was no power in Europe capable of stopping them. But then Ogedei died and the Mongols retreated.

Under their new leader Mongke, the Mongols captured Baghdad in 1258 and would have overrun the rest of the Islamic world had not Mongke also died. His successor was Kublai Khan, but he was less warlike and spent his life uniting the vast country of China. He allowed the Mongol Empire to break up into smaller sections.

At its height in 1279, the Mongol Empire stretched from the Baltic Sea to the Pacific Ocean, and from the Persian Gulf to the Arctic Circle. It was the biggest empire the world had ever seen.

▲ The Mongols were excellent riders and were able to cover up to 160 kilometres a day on their small and speedy horses. They fought with sharp arrows that could penetrate armour.

▼ In 1271, the Venetian traveller Marco Polo left Venice to visit China. He stayed in China for 20 years and met Kublai Khan, its ruler. Below is an illustration from the book he wrote about his travels. It shows gifts beings presented to 'the Great Khan'.

450–1450

The map shows locations including Baltic Sea, RUSSIA, Kiev, AUSTRIA, HUNGARY, Baghdad, EGYPT, Persian Gulf, KASHMIR, TIBET, INDIA, MONGOLIA, Peking, CHINA, Sung Empire (conquered 1279), JAPAN, PACIFIC OCEAN.

▲ The Mongol Empire was the largest empire the world had ever seen. At its greatest extent it stretched across Asia into eastern Europe and sent expeditions of conquest into Austria, Egypt, India, Java and Japan.

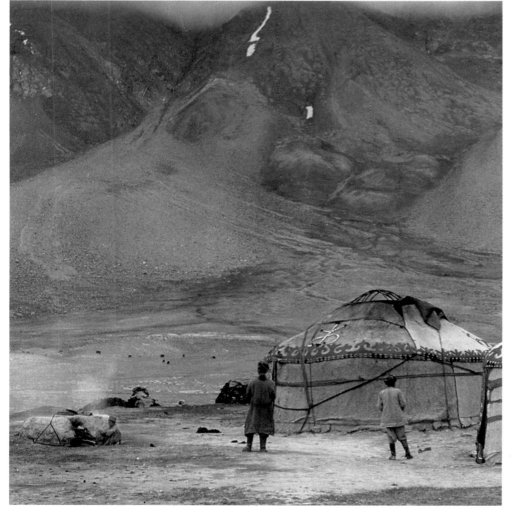

◀ The Mongols lived in yurts, or tents. The yurts were made of skins or woven cloth stretched over a wooden frame and they were decorated with brightly coloured rugs. They may not look strong but they were warm enough to keep out the cold of winter. Some tribes in Afghanistan still live in yurts today.

69

The Growth of Trade

Wars in Europe

In 1200 Europe was divided quite differently from how it is today. Spain was divided into four different countries, one of which, Granada, was ruled by the Moors of north Africa. Some areas of France were ruled by the kings of England, while Germany, the Netherlands, Switzerland, Austria and northern Italy were all part of the Holy Roman Empire. Italy was divided into many small city-states, while in eastern Europe the constant wars meant that the borders of the countries were always changing.

The most powerful ruler in western Europe was the **Pope** As the head of the Roman Catholic Church, the Pope ruled over the wealthiest organization in western Europe. The Church had vast amounts of land, with estates in many different countries, and everybody was a member of the Roman Catholic Church. The Pope therefore had great influence over how the various European countries conducted their affairs.

This vast power brought the Pope into conflict with the Holy Roman Emperor, who claimed to be the leader of western Europe. The Pope had the right to crown the Emperor and used this right to assert his superiority over the Emperor and all other rulers. But the Emperor wanted to be

English possessions in France in 1189

▲ In 1200, Europe was a patchwork of different states that were often at war with each other. The Holy Roman Empire consisted of numerous small states held together by the Holy Roman Emperor and the Pope. Quarrels between these two powerful rulers dominated European history at this time.

▶ In order to govern their countries better, many European kings summoned parliaments. These meetings were composed of nobles and other high-ranking people from each town. They levied (collected) taxes on behalf of the king and helped him administer the country. The English parliament (right) was summoned by Edward the First in 1295 and consisted of two knights from each county and two representatives from each town.

The Black Death

The Black Death

The Black Death was a plague spread by fleas which lived on both rats and humans. No one knows where the plague started, but it was probably brought from Asia into Europe by rat-infested ships that traded across the Mediterranean. The plague arrived in Sicily in 1347 and then spread slowly northwards throughout the rest of Europe, reaching Scandinavia by 1353. Its effect was devastating. Almost everyone who caught the plague – perhaps one third of the total population of Europe – died. Whole towns and villages were wiped out and harvests were left to rot in the fields. Only a few areas were unaffected, because they managed to isolate themselves and prevent the rats from spreading the disease.

▼ The Black Death killed almost everybody who caught it. It was often portrayed in pictures of the time as a dead person riding a horse, killing both rich and poor as it swept across the land.

▲ The Black Death probably came from Asia to Europe in 1347. It was carried by fleas that lived on rats, and on humans.

The Peasants' Revolt

Many other disasters struck Europe after 1300. A series of bad harvests led to widespread famine. Outbreaks of smallpox and influenza killed many people. Food prices rose because there were fewer people working on the land to produce the food. Across Europe, peasants demanded higher wages and violent demonstrations broke out in many countries. The most serious was in England, where wages were held down by law. In 1380, taxes were increased and many peasants revolted. Led by Wat Tyler, the peasants marched on London in 1381 and demanded changes in their working conditions. But Wat Tyler was killed and the revolt was put down with great severity.

71

independent of the Pope. As a result, the two frequently quarrelled and at times fighting broke out between them.

Daily life

The quarrel between the Holy Roman Emperor and the Pope had little impact on the daily lives of most men and women. For them, the most important thing was to produce enough food to eat.

At this time, almost everybody lived and worked on the land under a system known as the **Feudal System**, from the Latin word *feudum* meaning 'control'. The feudal system began in France in about 750 and soon spread across Europe. Each king granted land to his most powerful **barons** or lords, who swore an oath of loyalty and agreed to fight for the king if he needed their support. The barons then divided this land into manors.

The one group of people who did not own any land were the **villeins** or peasants. The lords of the manor gave the peasants strips of land to farm for themselves, but in return they had to work in their master's fields, and give him some of their produce each year. The peasants grew crops such as wheat, barley and beans, and grazed pigs. The Feudal System survived in Russia and eastern Europe until the 1800s. In western Europe, however, it began to collapse in the 1300s when more and more people began to work in the towns where the Feudal System did not apply.

▲ The first modern European bank was established in Venice in 1171 in order to lend money to the government. Banks were soon formed in every major European city, for they helped develop trade and commerce. Merchants used the banks to deposit and invest their money safely.

◄ The most important building in people's lives was the church. Everyone went to church and the local priest was often the most important member of the community. In bigger towns and cities, cathedrals were built to show off the wealth and power of the church. These cathedrals took many years to build and employed numerous local craftworkers. Stonemasons, wood carvers and glassmakers all helped decorate the cathedral with sculptures and coloured glass.

► Harvesting was a laborious task, requiring every man, woman and child to help. The barley or rye that was harvested went to make bread for the peasants, who also lived on eggs, cheese, milk and the occasional chicken or pig. The nobles ate much better, and used wheat for their bread.

▼ In this gold and silver mine in central Europe, the miners are shown wearing white so that they can be seen in the dark. Above ground people crush and wash the minerals while others sell them (top) under the supervision of royal controllers.

▼ In the bigger houses, servants were employed to cook and clean. This lady of the manor is giving her orders to her kitchen staff.

▼ Lepers and disabled people were common sights in many towns and villages, begging for food.

The Hanseatic League

In Europe, towns only started to grow in size after about 1200 when the threat of nomadic invasions had gone. New towns grew up along the trade routes where roads met or rivers could be crossed, while old towns expanded in the shadows of great cathedrals or fortified castles. These towns grew rich on trade. Many of them held fairs or markets where merchants could buy and sell their goods. Groups of craftworkers, such as goldsmiths or carpenters, formed associations known as **guilds** to protect their craft and train apprentices in their skills. These guilds grew rich and contributed much to the wealth of the towns.

In northern Europe, trade was dominated by the German towns around the south of the Baltic Sea. But this trade was often threatened by pirates at sea and robbers on land. In 1241, two of the towns, Hamburg and Lübeck, agreed to protect each other's merchants and safeguard their trade routes by setting up a *hanse*, or trading association. By 1300 all the German ports had set up hanses. Together they formed the Hanseatic League to safeguard their trading interests.

In 1400, at its greatest extent, the Hanseatic League had more than 150 members and traded throughout northern Europe. The Hanseatic traders brought copper, iron and herrings from Sweden and furs, grain and timber from eastern Europe and Russia. To the east, the

▲ Trade routes of the Hanseatic League. The Hanseatic League was the most important trading association in Europe. Its member towns stretched from Russia to Flanders and controlled trade in both the North and Baltic Seas.

▼ In the 1400s the fortified city of Novgorod in Russia was an important trading centre of the Hanseatic League. Amber, furs and wax were all traded here.

Inventions and Technology

Inventions came about over the course of many years as new ideas were used to improve old methods of working. Many of these inventions developed in China over hundreds of years and then slowly made their way to Europe, often through Arab influences. But printing and gunpowder remained unknown in Europe for many years after their first use in China, while the Chinese armies had no knowledge of the deadly longbow used by the English.

▲ The Diamond Sutra was printed in China in 868 and is the oldest surviving printed book in the world. The book is a collection of Buddhist prayers.

◄ The longbow was developed in England in the 1200s and was a lethal weapon because of the speed and accuracy of its delivery.

▼ The padded horse collar was originally a Chinese invention, introduced into Europe in the 900s. It enabled horses to be used on farms to pull heavy loads. Here a horse wearing a padded collar is pulling a harrow.

▼ The Chinese were skilled iron workers. Here a group of workers are forging a ship's anchor in the 1300s.

merchants or traders of the League controlled the town of Novgorod in Russia, and dominated trade in that country. To the west, they traded across the North Sea with England. There the traders were known as *Easterlings*, because they came from the east. In time the word became shortened to 'sterling' and referred to the money the Hanse traders used. The word sterling is still in use today as the name for British currency.

Southern Europe

Venice was the most important trading city in southern Europe. As early as 900, the Venetians controlled most of the trade with the Middle East and China. They profited by equipping the fleets and armies that went on the Crusades, and by 1400 Venice had established an empire of trading ports throughout the eastern Mediterranean Sea. In this way it became the richest city in Europe.

China

In China too, towns were growing in size and importance. The population of China had reached over 110 million people by 1100, many more than lived in the whole of Europe. Cities such as Kaifeng became important trading and industrial centres, and by 1450 China had become the richest and most organized country in the world.

Opposite: Part of a European map printed in 1570. The complete map shows the Americas and Africa

▲ For many years traders to the Middle East and China started their journeys from Venice. By 1400 it was a thriving port and the richest commercial city in Europe.

▼ Between 960 and 1127, the Chinese capital was at Kaifeng. It had a population of perhaps one million people and was a major centre of trade and industry. This scroll, drawn in about 1120, shows the bustle of the annual Spring Festival.

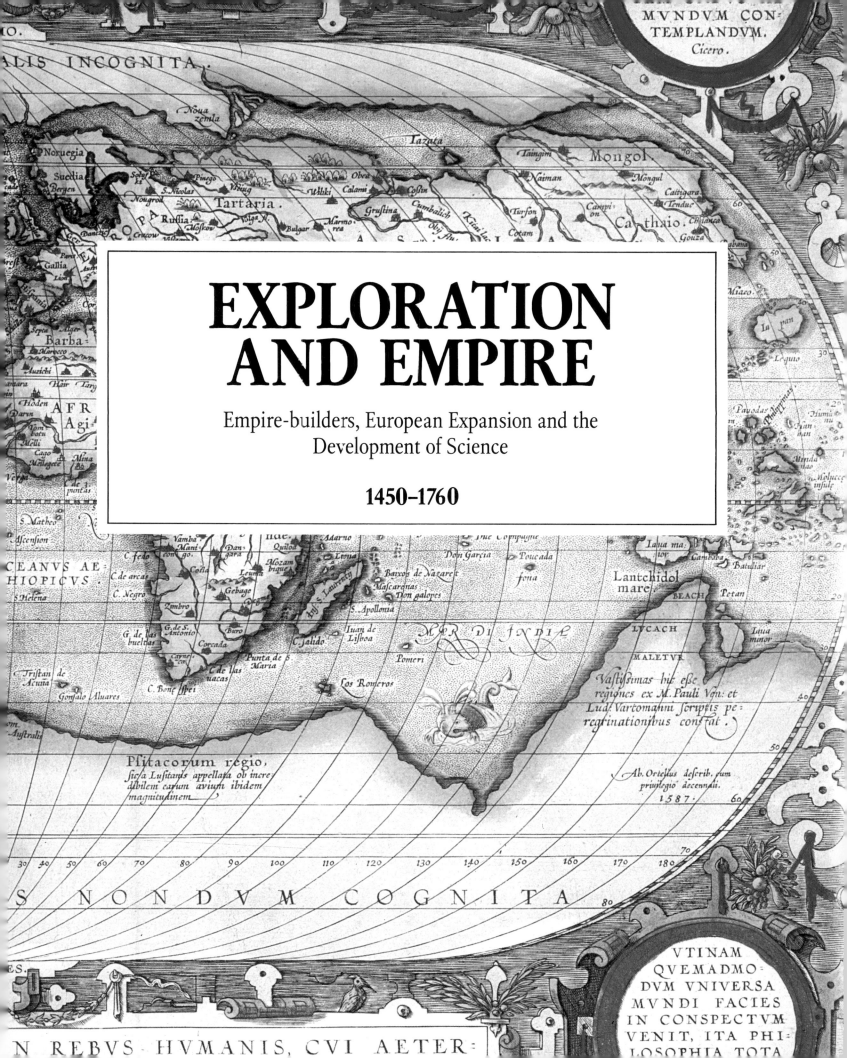

EXPLORATION AND EMPIRE

Empire-builders, European Expansion and the
Development of Science

1450–1760

Exploration and Empire

Old and new

Today we live in a world of fast travel and instant communication. But in 1450 most people never traveled farther than their own town or village. Others did not know that countries existed beyond their own. Great civilizations rose and flourished almost independently of each other.

Western Europe, which influences so much of our lives today, was on the edge of the civilized world in 1450. All around the world, civilizations such as the Mughal Empire in India, the Ming Dynasty in China, and the brilliant Aztec and Inca Empires in central and south America flourished. In west Africa the Kingdom of Benin rose to its height and in Australia the Aboriginal culture continued to flourish as it had done for many thousands of years, independent of any contact with the outside world.

Toward one world

But the world was poised on the brink of great change. Between 1450 and 1750 European seafarers, traders, and **colonists** set out to explore and exploit the rest of the world. This brought the continents into direct contact with each other for the first time. From 1450 the history of the world begins to move from

▲ **The North American Indians:** the Thunderbird was a mythical creature with an extra head on its front.

▲ **The Aztecs:** the Aztec god Quetzalcoatl "the Plumed Serpent." The Aztecs dominated central America in the 1400s. They had an efficient system of administration and ran the country from their vast capital at Tenochtitlán.

▶ **The Incas:** a silver llama—one of the few pieces of Inca metalwork that was not destroyed by the Spanish after their invasion. The Incas governed a vast empire in south America of over six million people.

▶ **The Ming Dynasty:** an official of the Ming Dynasty finely carved in ivory. The Ming Dynasty ruled China from 1368 to 1644, creating a rich and powerful state.

EUROPE

ASIA

Ottoman Empire

Persian
Safavid Empire

Mughal
Empire

Chinese
Ming Dynasty

PACIFIC OCEAN

Songhai/Mali Empires
Kingdom of Benin

AFRICA

INDIAN OCEAN

AUSTRALIA
Aborigines

◀ **The Kingdom of
Benin:** the Kingdom of
Benin flourished in west
Africa from the 1300s to
the 1600s. It was famous
for its beautiful sculptures
elaborately cast in bronze.

▶ **The Australian
Aborigines:** the
Aborigine people had for
10,000 years hunted and
gathered food over a wide
area, developing their own
entirely separate culture.

79

being the story of different civilizations to the history of one, interconnected world.

New ways of thinking

As we have seen, Europe in 1450 was not the richest or the most important region of the world. But it was a place where important changes were occurring. During the 1400s and 1500s there were great advances in the arts and sciences, and the beginnings of new and exciting ways of thinking about the world and human nature.

This period in European history is called the **Renaissance** (meaning *rebirth*). It began in northern Italy where wealthy and educated people began to take a renewed interest in the art and literature of Ancient Greece and Rome. This led to great artistic achievements by people such as Michelangelo, Raphael, and Leonardo da Vinci. It also stimulated interest in learning and a new spirit of inquiry, influenced by ideas from the Islamic world. The science of astronomy was developed, and there were advances in medicine. Scholars and thinkers began to challenge the rigid teaching of the medieval Church.

Helped by the invention of printing, the ideas and scholarship of the Renaissance gradually spread throughout Europe. The Renaissance only affected the wealthiest and most privileged in society but it provided a stimulus to the European urge to explore and discover the world outside.

▶ The Renaissance started among the many city-states of northern Italy. Here, art and architecture were paid for by wealthy and educated people, including women like Isabella d'Este (*below*) who took a personal interest in the new learning.

Milan • Verona •
Padua • Venice •
Mantua •
Modena • Bologna •
Ravenna •
Pisa • Florence •
Urbino •
Siena •

ITALY

Rome ■

0   50 miles
0   50 Kilometers

◀ Leonardo da Vinci was a painter, sculptor, architect, and engineer. Among his many drawings was an idea for a flying machine, devised 400 years before the first aircraft, and this parachute.

▲ The city of Florence was one of the main centres of the Italian Renaissance, with many rich **patrons** supporting artists and architects.

The Invention of Printing

Today we take newspapers and books for granted. But until the 1450s information was either passed from one person to another by word of mouth or copied and written out laboriously by hand. In the 1450s a German craftsman, Johannes Gutenberg, introduced the printing press into Europe. It revolutionized communication. For the first time books or "broadsheets" could be produced quickly and easily, which meant that more people than ever before had access to learning and ideas.

The Bible and classical texts were the first books to be printed in Europe. By 1520, there were more than 200 different printed editions of the Bible in several different languages. Printing was also used to spread the new scientific and political ideas of the Renaissance.

▼ Gutenberg's press, which was adapted from a wine press of the time, used movable metal type for the first time. Earlier printers carved groups of letters onto a woodblock; but individual letters cast in molds could be moved and used over and over again. The type was inked, and then separate sheets of paper, one at a time, were placed on top of the wet type. In this way whole books could be reproduced thousands of times.

▲ The first European printing press was set up, by Gutenberg, in Mainz in what is now Germany in 1454. Over the next 50 years printing presses were introduced into Germany, Italy, France, Spain, and England.

▲ The *Ladies Mercury*, one of the early broadsheets, which was printed and distributed widely.

Exploration and the Scramble for Riches

From around 1450 European sailors and navigators set out on remarkable voyages of exploration. Curiosity was one reason, the search for trade and wealth was another.

Overland trade routes had existed between Europe and Asia for centuries, along which merchants had brought spices, silks and gems from the East to Europe. But in 1453 when the Ottoman Turks captured Constantinople (Istanbul) direct land links between Europe and Asia were cut completely. It became essential to find a sea route to the East.

In the 1460s the Portuguese explored the west coast of Africa, setting up forts and trading in gold, ivory and silver. In 1488 Bartolomeu Dias reached the Cape of Good Hope. In 1498 Vasco da Gama was the first European to reach India by sea.

A 'new world'

While the Portuguese were sailing east, the Spanish were exploring the oceans to the west. In 1492 Christopher Columbus set off to find India by sailing west. He 'discovered' the Caribbean Islands and, believing them to be part of Asia, called them the West Indies. He went on to find South America, part of an entire continent unknown to the Europeans.

▲ Claudius Ptolemy drew his map of the world in the AD100s and it was rediscovered by Europeans in the 1400s. Using this map, the first Europeans to reach America believed that it must be part of Asia because the new continent was not on the map.

▶ The European exploration of the world was made possible by a new and faster type of ship, the *caravel*, developed by the Portuguese. Nevertheless, sailing into the unknown was a frightening experience, and many of the sailors believed that monsters would threaten them while at sea.

▲ Columbus's ship, the *Santa Maria*. Life aboard the *Santa Maria* was very tough – there was no sleeping accommodation for the crew and their food was cooked in an open pot on deck.

Amerigo Vespucci explored the South American coast down to the mouth of the Amazon. The previously unnamed continent in the **'New World'** was called America after him.

Between 1519 and 1522 **Ferdinand Magellan** proved that the world's oceans were linked by sailing around the world – but only 18 of his crew of 250 survived the voyage.

In 1498 **Vasco da Gama** became the first European to sail to India, in a voyage that took him around the coast of Africa.

Barents 1596-97

Cabot 1497

EUROPE

ASIA

● Constantinople

Overland routes blocked by Muslim states

CHINA

NORTH AMERICA

ATLANTIC OCEAN

Columbus 1492

INDIA

Philippines

West Indies

Calicut

FIC OCEAN

Vespucci 1499-1500

AFRICA

East Indies

The Moluccas

Da Gama 1497-99

Janszoon 1605

Diaz 1487-88

INDIAN OCEAN

SOUTH AMERICA

Magellan 1519-22

Tasman 1642-44

Cape of Good Hope

Strait of Magellan

Cape Horn

In 1492 **Christopher Columbus** became the first European to reach the Caribbean, landing in the Bahamas. He later explored the South American coast.

In 1497 **John Cabot** became the first European to sail to North America since the Vikings, 500 years before. He explored Newfoundland and Canada.

Cheng Ho
Almost a century before the Europeans sailed into the Indian Ocean, the Chinese Ming rulers sent seven expeditions to explore this area. Commanded by Cheng Ho, vast fleets explored as far afield as east Africa, the Red Sea, Persia, India and Java. They brought back gifts from the local rulers, rare spices and unusual animals, including lions and giraffes.

Compass

Astrolabe

Backstaff

▲ Navigation at sea was a very primitive affair in the 1500s. The most important instrument was the compass which told which direction the ship was sailing in. The **astrolabe** and backstaff used the sun to calculate the ship's distance north or south of the Equator. Sailors had no accurate way of finding out how far east or west they went until the mid-1700s, when the chronometer was perfected.

83

Gold, guns, and disease

Explorers and navigators were followed by **conquistadors** and colonists in search of land and gold for their countries. The Spanish first occupied the Caribbean and then turned their attention to South and Central America, which were rich in gold and silver.

When the Spanish arrived in Central and South America they found two great civilizations—the Aztecs of Mexico and the Incas of Peru. Both were highly organized societies of millions of people. The Aztecs had developed astronomy, methods of irrigation and a highly diverse agriculture, growing crops such as corn, tobacco, potatoes, and tomatoes which the Europeans later took back to Europe. Both Aztecs and Incas were highly skilled builders. Tenochtitlán, the Aztec capital which lay on Lake Texcoco, was larger than any European city of the time. Yet between 1519 and 1534 both empires were overthrown by the Spanish and their wealth and land seized.

The Spanish conquest was achieved by Hernán Cortés who overthrew Aztec rule between 1519 and 1521, and by Francisco Pizarro who conquered the Inca Empire between 1532 and 1534. Although the Spanish were few in number they brought guns and horses against which the American peoples had no defense. As a result the Spanish were able to capture the Aztec and Inca leaders very easily.

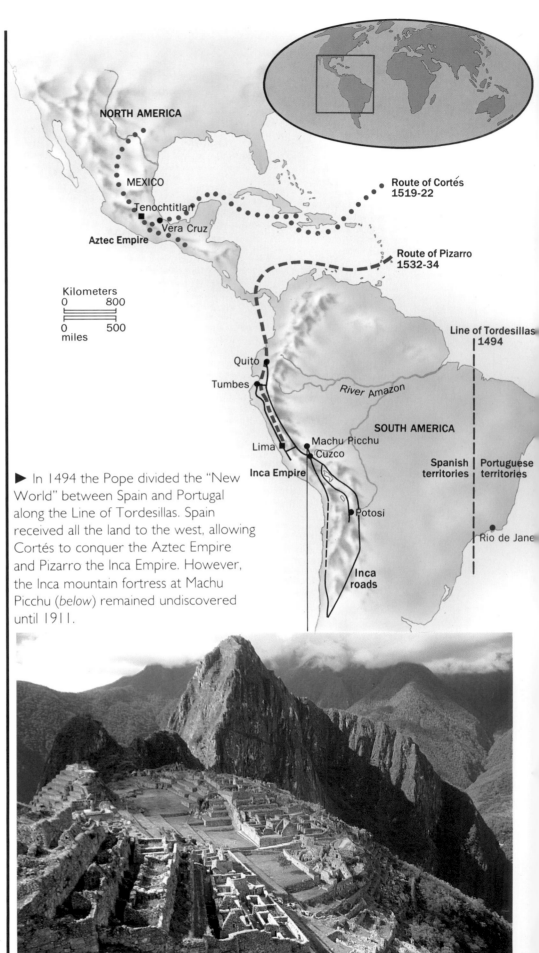

► In 1494 the Pope divided the "New World" between Spain and Portugal along the Line of Tordesillas. Spain received all the land to the west, allowing Cortés to conquer the Aztec Empire and Pizarro the Inca Empire. However, the Inca mountain fortress at Machu Picchu (*below*) remained undiscovered until 1911.

84

▲ In order to exploit the gold and silver of the "New World," the Spanish put the native Americans to work in the mines. Conditions were harsh and many thousands died.

▶ When the first Europeans arrived in the Aztec Empire in 1519, its ruler Montezuma believed them to be gods and welcomed them into the capital, showering them with gifts.

◀ This snake, made of hollow wood covered with turquoise, was made by Aztec craftspeople and probably sent as a tribute to Tenochtitlán. It was worn at the back of the head as part of a headdress.

▼ The central part of the great Aztec city, Tenochtitlán. The city was begun in 1325 and built on an island on Lake Texcoco.

When the Spanish began to conquer South America in 1519, the native population was about 57 million. By 1607, this had dropped to just over 4 million. Some of this decline was due to warfare and harsh conditions in the mines, but much of it was because of the introduction of European diseases, such as measles, smallpox, and chickenpox, against which the native peoples had no **immunity**.

Temple of Huitzilopochtli

Priests' quarters

Sacrificial skull-rack

Temple of the Sun

The scramble for riches

By the mid-1550s the Spanish and Portuguese had established the first European overseas empires. They set up **plantations** in the Caribbean and colonized large areas of South America. In 1510 the Portuguese captured Goa in India. In the 1540s they became the first Europeans to land in Japan. By the 1550s they controlled trade in the Indian Ocean and the **Spice Islands**. But from the late 1500s onward **The Netherlands**, France, and England began to challenge Spain and Portugal and to compete with them for trade, in spices and slaves.

England was already a great sea power and trading nation. As well as trading for slaves in the Caribbean, English pirates and sailors such as Francis Drake raided the Spanish colonies in the Americas, plundering their ships and carrying off gold, silver, and other treasure. In 1588 Philip the Second of Spain sent an armed fleet — the **Armada** — to attack England, but the Spanish fleet failed in its task. This weakened Spain's empire and led to the growth of British power overseas.

The Dutch too were a prosperous nation. They drove the Portuguese out of the Spice Islands and in 1658 they captured Ceylon (Sri Lanka). By the 1680s they had built up their own empire in Southeast Asia. By 1650 the European nations had established a sea-trading network that stretched as far as India.

▼ By 1650 Portugal, Spain, England, The Netherlands, and France had built up trading empires overseas, although their influence was usually confined to coastal areas.

Portuguese   French
Spanish   Dutch
British

▶ From the 1460s onward the Portuguese established a series of trading posts around the coast of Africa, including this one at Elmina in west Africa.

▼ The European invasion of the "New World" was often opposed, and the local peoples continued to fight the invaders for years. In 1608 the **Caribs** of St. Lucia fought against the British colonists.

The Spice Trade

When the Portuguese reached the East Indies in the early 1500s, they found the islands rich in spices unobtainable in Europe. The Portuguese quickly took control of this lucrative trade by conquering the Moluccas and seizing the main ports in the Indian Ocean and China through which the spice trade passed.

For almost a century, the Portuguese controlled the spice trade with Europe, but by 1600, both England and The Netherlands had established East India Companies to obtain spices directly for themselves. The Dutch were the most successful, driving the Portuguese out of the Moluccas and keeping the English out of the region altogether. They encouraged the growing of tea, coffee, sugar, and tobacco on the islands, and by 1720 they had become the main coffee suppliers to Europe.

▲ Harvesting pepper cloves in the Spice Islands.

▲ Pepper is used to season food and flavor soups and gravies.

▲ Nutmeg is used to flavor custards and milk puddings.

▲ Cloves are used to flavor food, particularly meat.

▲ Between 1618 and 1629, the Dutch expelled the Portuguese from the Spice Islands and established a vast empire with its capital at Batavia (Jakarta).

▲ Mace is used in pickles and hot mulled wines.

Religion and Change

In the early 1500s the Christian Roman Catholic Church was the main religion in Europe. The Church was the most powerful force in society: it dominated people's thinking. But within 50 years, almost half the population of western Europe had left the Roman Catholic Church to worship in rival Christian Churches. This change is called the Reformation. It resulted from a protest about the corruption of the Roman Catholic Church and its priests, and a demand for reform.

In 1517 a German monk called Martin Luther wrote a list of 95 'theses', or complaints, which were printed and circulated throughout Europe. The Church refused to consider reform and Luther was **excommunicated**, or expelled, from the Roman Catholic Church in 1520. Luther then set up his own reformed Church in Saxony. Similar Churches were soon established in the rest of Germany and northern Europe.

In order to regain control of Europe, in 1545 the Roman Catholic Church began to reform itself, in a movement called the Counter-Reformation. The Counter-Reformation led to bitter civil wars, and a general European war that lasted 30 years from 1618 to 1648.

Europe in 1560

☐ Roman Catholic

▨ Protestant

Boundary between Roman Catholic and Greek and Russian Orthodox churches

SCOTLAND
SWEDEN
IRELAND
ENGLAND
• Wittenberg
POLAND
SAXONY
• Paris
• Worms
FRANCE
SWISS CANTONS
Geneva
HUNGARY
•Genoa
OTTOMAN EMPIRE
Muslim
PORTUGAL
SPAIN
Rome

▲ By 1560 the people of Europe were divided by their religion. Those who broke away from the power of the Roman Catholic Church are shown as Protestants on the map – in fact there were many different new movements, the Anglicans in England, the New Lutherans and the Calvinists for example. In the east the Russian and Greek Orthodox Christian Churches had long been established, and in the south-east, the Ottoman Empire was Muslim in faith.

▶ Martin Luther. His followers were called Protestants because they protested against the Roman Catholic Church.

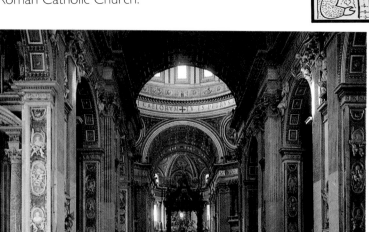

▼ Inside St Peter's in Rome, the centre of the Roman Catholic Church.

◄ The Calvinist Church was based on the severe and strict teachings of John Calvin, a Frenchman living in Geneva. Its buildings were stark in comparison with the decorative Roman Catholic churches.

▼ From 1562 to 1598, France was split by religious wars between Roman Catholics and Huguenots, or Protestants of the Calvinist Church. The Roman Catholic Queen, Catherine de Medici, ordered all the Huguenots to be killed on St Bartholomew's Day in 1572. Over 29,000 were murdered.

Henry the Eighth of England
In England, Henry the Eighth wanted to divorce his wife, Catherine of Aragon, because she had failed to produce a male heir to the throne. The Roman Catholic Church would not agree, so Henry made himself head of the new Anglican Church and granted his own divorce. He dissolved the monasteries, the richest landowners in the country, and seized their wealth, increasing his own power.

89

Rich and poor

In the 1500s and 1600s in Europe the vast majority of people lived off the land. Famine, poverty and disease were common and few people lived past the age of 40. Most remained poor and uneducated, lacking the knowledge or equipment to farm efficiently. The weather and harvest were the most crucial aspects of their lives.

But changes were taking place that gradually altered people's lives. Between 1500 and 1700 the population of Europe grew steadily, leading to pressure for more efficient and productive farming. In some countries, such as England, wealthy local landowners began to enclose open fields and **common land** in order to make higher profits: they turned **arable** land into pasture for sheep, and threw the peasant farmers off the land.

In the towns rich merchants were profiting from increased trade and commerce throughout Europe and with the rest of the world. With their new-found wealth they invested their money in the new banks set up to finance the growing **merchant economy**. Many rich people were also commissioning fine buildings and works of art, particularly in The Netherlands, which by 1650 was the richest country in Europe. The growth of the new merchant class, dedicated to business and profit, meant that by 1650 the gap between rich and poor had become very wide.

▲ The first ploughs had a single wedge, tipped with iron, that could only break the surface of the soil, not turn it. By the middle of the 1600s double ploughs were in use throughout Europe. These new ploughs were able to turn the soil and to prepare it better for planting the crops.

▼ Most people who lived in the 1500s and 1600s were poor, living on the land and dependent on a good harvest for their livelihood. This painting by Breughel shows the living room of a Flemish farmer in the early 1600s. A rich nobleman and his wife bring presents of salt and money to the farmer's family.

The Potato

In 1500 the potato grew in the Andes mountains of South America and the only people who ate it were the Incas. Their Spanish conquerors introduced it into Europe in the middle of the 1500s, but it was about 200 years before it became the popular food in Europe that it is today. In about 1600, the potato was taken back across the Atlantic by settlers who introduced it to North America.

Nuns, Witches and Dissenters

Life was hard for most women during this period because by law women had few rights. Their lives and their fortunes were controlled by their fathers or, if they were married, by their husbands. Most women worked in the fields and brought up many children.

Some unmarried women entered convents as nuns. In 1535 one nun, Angela Merici, founded a teaching order, the Ursulines who later emigrated to North America and set up the first convent in Quebec in 1639. Other older women were herbalists or wise women who tended the sick in the villages. Many people were very suspicious of these women, who suffered and were persecuted as witches during the 1400s and 1500s.

Women also played some part in the political and social changes of the time. In Italy and France a number of notable women, such as Lucrezia Borgia and the artist Artesemia Gemileschi, played a leading role in the new learning. By the 1600s some women were beginning to demand women's rights. In England during a time of political and religious dissent in the 1640s a pamphlet appeared. It was called *The Women's Sharpe Revenge*. Written by two women who called themselves Mary Tattle-well and Joan Hit-him-home, it attacked the critics of women and was an early demand for women's rights.

▲ The Quakers were a religious group which began in the mid-1600s in England. They were also known as the Society of Friends. They believed that men and women were equal – this picture shows a woman preaching at a meeting.

▼ In Europe in the 1400s and 1500s, thousands of women were accused of being witches and tortured and burned as a result.

▼ Noblewomen did have certain traditional rights in the 1400s and 1500s, but from the 1600s onwards these were gradually taken away. Lady Anne Clifford was an English noblewoman who fought against the loss of these rights.

The Ottoman Empire

To the east of Europe lay one of the largest and most successful empires in the world – the Ottoman Empire. It had been founded by Muslim Turks in the late 1200s. Under their king, Osman the First, from whom the empire took its name, the Ottomans managed to exploit the weaknesses and divisions of their neighbours and establish dominance over Anatolia (Turkey) and then farther afield in Europe, Asia and Africa. Their greatest triumph came in 1453 when they captured the great Christian city of Constantinople, capital of the Byzantine Empire.

They renamed this city Istanbul and made it the capital of their vast empire. At its greatest extent in 1566, the Ottoman Empire covered more than two and a half million square kilometres, from Algeria to Arabia and from Budapest to Cairo. In 1529 and again in 1683, the Ottomans even reached the capital of the Holy Roman Empire, Vienna, in the heart of Europe, but were unable to capture it.

Throughout most of the 1500s, the Ottoman Empire was at war with its neighbour, the Safavid Empire of Persia (Iran). Like Christian Europe, the Muslim world was divided, for while the Ottomans were of the Sunni sect, the Safavids fought many wars because of their religious differences, and over the possession of territory. This dispute still continues today.

Ottoman Empire

▲ At its greatest extent in 1566, the Ottoman Empire covered the whole of the Middle East, north Africa and much of south-east Europe. To its west lay Christian Europe, while to its east was the Muslim Safavid Empire of Persia.

In order to fight their many wars, the Ottomans had a highly-trained army led by Janissaries (*above*). Distinguished by their tall plumed hats, these élite troops were Christians, captured or recruited from Europe. Ottoman women, however, were considered little better than the servants employed by each rich household. This Turkish lady and her servant are on the way to the baths (*right*).

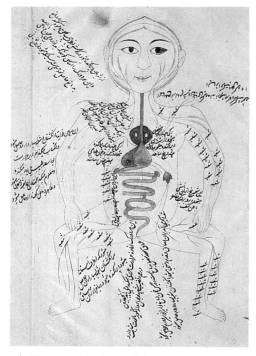

▲ The study of medicine was very advanced in the Islamic world. This Persian manuscript of the 1600s shows an understanding of the human organs and the circulation of the blood.

▶ Suleiman brought Ottoman power to its peak when he brought his armies to the gates of Vienna. He is seen here at the Battle of Mohács in 1526, when he defeated the Hungarian army. *Upper centre:* Suleiman rides his horse through a pile of dead bodies. *Lower corner:* defeated Hungarians flee on horseback.

After the capture of Constantinople in 1453, the Ottomans renamed the city Istanbul and made it their capital. Minarets were built on to the Christian church of St Sophia and it was turned into a mosque (*below and left*).

The Mughal Empire

At the same time as the Ottoman Turks and the Persian Safavids were establishing their empires, a third empire was being founded in India. All three were Islamic. Together they ensured that by the 1500s the Islamic world was far larger than the Christian.

The Islamic empire in India was founded in 1504 when a group of Turks led by Babur captured Kabul in Afghanistan. Babur claimed descent from the Mongol ruler Genghis Khan; from the word Mongol came Mughal. Babur soon moved south into the fertile plains of northern India and in 1526 his army of 12,000 defeated a 100,000-strong Indian army. Establishing their capital at Delhi, Babur and his successors spread Mughal rule over most of India by the mid-1600s.

Although the Mughals were Muslims, four-fifths of their subjects were Hindus who were at first allowed to practice their religion unhindered. But by the 1700s the Hindus were being persecuted, leading to strains within the Empire that eventually led to its break-up.

A further threat came from the fact that the Mughals had never had much interest in the sea or overseas trade, allowing Europeans, notably the Portuguese, to establish trading ports around the coast as early as 1510. These ports soon developed into bases for European powers seeking to expand their own trading and colonial empires abroad.

▲ In 1650, at the height of its power, the Mughal Empire covered almost all of present-day India, Pakistan, and Bangladesh. Many of its coastal towns were occupied by Europeans, notably the Portuguese, Dutch, French, and English.

▲ Although the Mughals were Muslims, they tolerated other religions within their empire, notably the Sikhs. The Golden Temple in the city of Amritsar is the holiest shrine of the Sikh religion.

94

The first European settlements in India were founded not by countries but by trading companies, such as the British East India Company. Set up in 1600 with a charter from Elizabeth I of England to trade with the East, it soon acquired many privileges from the Mughals, employing local women (*above*) to produce cotton for export and planting large estates with tea (*right*) to satisfy the British thirst for the drink.

▼ When Babur became Mughal Emperor, he complained that India had no grapes, good fruits, or cold water. He therefore encouraged the building of beautiful gardens.

▼ Built as a mausoleum (tomb) for Mumtaz, the favorite wife of Emperor Shah Jahan, the Taj Mahal took 20,000 builders 18 years to complete. It was finally ready in 1648.

95

Slavery and the New World

Quebec
• Montreal

1

2

3
• Boston

4

5

6

7

• New York

ATLANTIC OCEAN

Philadelphia

8

Baltimore 9

Indian Reserve

10

• Jamestown

French Louisiana

11

12

13

Spanish Florida

THE 13 COLONIES
1 New Hampshire 1680
2 New York 1664
3 Massachusetts 1629
4 Connecticut 1636
5 Rhode Island 1635
6 Pennsylvania 1681
7 New Jersey 1664
8 Maryland 1632
9 Delaware 1702
10 Virginia 1607
11 N. Carolina 1670
12 S. Carolina 1670
13 Georgia 1732

A hundred years or so after Columbus arrived in the Americas, people from all over Europe began to cross the Atlantic to settle in what they called the 'New World'. The Portuguese and Spanish concentrated on Central and South America and the Caribbean. There they mined for silver and set up vast plantations which were worked by slave labour, growing profitable crops, such as tobacco, sugar and cotton.

The French, Dutch and British concentrated on North America. In 1535 the Frenchman, Jacques Cartier, sailed up the St Lawrence River and established a port at Montreal in what is now Canada. French influence then extended into central North America, which the French called Louisiana after their king, Louis the Fourteenth.

In 1607 the British set up their first American colony at Jamestown in Virginia. They continued to colonize the Atlantic coast, expelling the Dutch from New York in 1664, and by 1700 more than 250,000 English people were living in North America. They organized their settlements into 12 colonies, a thirteenth, Georgia, being formed in 1732. These 13 colonies eventually formed the first states of the United States of America.

Tobacco
Colonists in Virginia grew tobacco – a plant native to South America. It was taken to Europe where smoking soon became popular. In the early 1600s, James the First of England described tobacco as 'loathsome to the eyes, hateful to the nose, harmful to the braine, dangerous to the lung . . .'

1535–1760

A chiefe Herowans wyfe of Pomeoc.
and her daughter of the age of, 8. or.
10. yeares.

▲ The native tribes of North America lived by hunting and trapping wild animals for their fur and meat. In this picture the native Americans camouflage themselves in order to stalk their prey. At first this way of life was unaffected by the arrival of the Europeans. But gradually the two groups came into bitter conflict as the native Americans were driven from their land by the expanding European colonies.

▶ One of the first settlers in North America was John White, a map-maker and artist, who drew pictures of the native Americans, including this one of a woman and her child.

Many of the first European colonists were dissenters, people who disagreed with the accepted religion in their country, and who were persecuted for their beliefs. One of these groups, the Pilgrim Fathers, was made up of Puritan men and women who disagreed with the English Anglican Church. They left England in 1620 on the *Mayflower* (*above*) and founded a settlement in Massachusetts.

A PURITAN FAMILY.

Settlers and Americans

The early European settlers found existing cultures already established on their arrival in the 'New World'. At that time North America contained many different tribes of native Americans, each with their own customs and ways of life. The first settlers met with little opposition, as their small numbers posed no threat to the local inhabitants, whom they named 'Indians'. The settlers needed the Indians to supply them with food and furs to supplement the unreliable deliveries from Europe and to help them through the harsh winters and years of crop failure. At the same time the Indians wanted to acquire arms to fight their local wars.

Local **alliances** soon sprung up, and in Canada, the French helped one Indian tribe, the Iroquois, to destroy another, the Huron, in 1649, while farther south similar alliances were forged between the British settlers and local Indian groups. These alliances divided the Indians and prevented a united Indian threat to the fledgling colonies.

But as the European colonies grew, they began to threaten the livelihood and independence of the Indians. The British colonists in Connecticut were attacked by the Pequot Indians in 1637, while all the New England colonies were involved in a war against the Wampanoag and Narragansett Indians in 1675–6, which led to the virtual destruction of tribal life in the area.

▲ The first European settlers built themselves simple log cabins able to withstand the cold winters they encountered in the 'New World'. But as they established themselves, they cleared more land and built bigger and more comfortable houses.

▼ The native Americans were experienced in trapping wild animals, especially beavers, for their skin and fur, which they traded with the European settlers for arms and other goods.

▼ In 1612 the Dutch settled on an island in the Hudson River and named the place New Amsterdam. When the English captured it in 1664, they renamed it New York. This map was drawn in 1664 and shows the English fleet in the harbour.

The Slave Trade

Between the 1400s and 1800s at least 10 million black Africans were shipped from Africa to labour on the sugar, tobacco and cotton plantations of the Caribbean and North America. The Portuguese were the first to practise this trade in human lives; later the British became the main slave traders. In a horrendous but profitable '**triangular trade**' ships sailed from Britain with manufactured goods which were exchanged for slaves on the west coast of Africa. Cargoes of slaves – women, men and children – were taken across the Atlantic (the 'middle passage') and then sold in the Caribbean and North and South America where most were worked to death on the plantations. The same ships then took the products of the plantations – cotton, raw sugar (known as white gold because it was so profitable) and tobacco – back to Europe where they were sold.

kilometres
0   1000
0   600
miles

Cotton, sugar, tobacco

EUROPE

NORTH AMERICA

Trade goods

WEST INDIES

AFRICA

Jamaica

Caribbean Sea

Slaves

Elmina

SOUTH AMERICA

◀ Many black Africans rebelled. The fighting **Maroons** of Jamaica were a colony of escaped slaves who, in 1739, forced the British to make a **treaty** with them.

▼ During the middle passage from Africa to the Americas hundreds of black Africans were crammed together on disease-ridden slave ships and transported across the Atlantic in appalling conditions. Many perished.

TO BE SOLD on board the Ship *Bance-Ifland*, on tuefday the 6th of *May* next, at *Afhley-Ferry*; a choice cargo of about 250 fine healthy

NEGROES,

juft arrived from the Windward & Rice Coaft. —The utmoft care has already been taken, and fhall be continued, to keep them free from the leaft danger of being infected with the SMALL-POX, no boat having been on board, and all other communication with people from *Charles-Town* prevented.

Aufin, Laurens, & Appleby.

N. B. Full one Half of the above Negroes have had the SMALL-POX in their own Country.

Africa

By the 1500s the African continent was home to many different political states and powerful kingdoms. Within the continent these societies had developed trade networks, advanced forms of agriculture, gold mining, cloth working, and a variety of crafts and skills. Contact between these states and the rest of the world was limited, for the Sahara Desert was an almost impassable barrier to all but the hardiest of traders. But the gradual spread of Islam across the desert linked Africa more closely to the Arab world and by the 1600s trade between Africa and the Mediterranean was well established.

The slave trade

The arrival of the Europeans interrupted African development. At first European settlement was limited to coastal areas as the Portuguese began to trade with west African kings for gold, ivory, pepper and cloth in exchange for goods, most of which were of little use to the Africans. Slaves also formed part of this trade. At first European demand for slaves was met by west African states where slavery existed as punishment for various crimes. But by the 1700s Europeans were buying or kidnapping slaves from the whole of Africa. The effect on African cultures was devastating and by the late 1700s the population had declined and many African states were seriously weakened.

BRANDING SLAVES,
ON THE COAST OF AFRICA PREVIOUS TO EMBARKATION.

▲ When a slave was captured, he or she was branded, as described in a contemporary French account, 'with a red-hot iron, imprinting the mark of the French, English or Dutch companies, so that each nation may distinguish its own. Care is taken that the women, as tenderest, be not burnt too hard.'

▶ An ivory carving from west Africa depicting Portuguese soldiers in a miniature ship's crow's nest.

▼ Built on an island off Tanzania, the town of Kilwa became the major trading port in east Africa in the 1200s, 'with many fair houses of stone and mortar,

surrounded by orchards and fruit gardens irrigated by fresh water.' In 1505 the Portuguese captured the town and built a fort to control it.

◀ The town of Timbuctu in the Songhai Empire of west Africa. Leo Africanus, a Muslim from Spain, visited Timbuctu early in the 1500s. He recorded that 'the rich King has many plates and sceptres of gold . . . Here are many doctors, judges, priests and other learned men. And here are brought different manuscripts and books . . . which are sold for more money than any other merchandise.

▼ The west African kingdom of Benin was famed for its bronze casting. The craftspeople even made statues of visiting Portuguese soldiers and musketeers.

Ottoman conquest

SAHARA DESERT

Nile River

Timbuctu
Songhai • Goa
River Niger
Katsina
• Kano
Dahomey
Hausa States
Ashanti
Elmina Accra Benin
Ethiopia

0   800 kilometres
0   500 miles

Luanda ○
Benguela ○

Luba
Lunda

Kilwa ○

○ European coastal settlements

Madagascar

Cape Town ○
Khoisan

◀ While African cultures such as the Luba, Ashanti and Hausa states continued to develop in the interior, the coastal peoples of Africa were affected by the arrival of the Europeans, particularly the Portuguese. Areas within the red lines were African kingdoms.

Struggles for Power

In 1648, the Peace of Westphalia brought to an end the Thirty Years War between the Catholic **Habsburg** emperors and their Protestant subjects in the Holy Roman Empire. It also marked an important turning point. European wars until 1648 had been fought mainly on religious grounds. Now different nations began to struggle amongst each other for political supremacy in Europe, and for trade and colonies abroad.

Between 1667 and 1714 France was involved in four major wars. At first these wars were to secure French frontiers in the east. But in 1700, when Charles the Second, King of Spain, died, it appeared possible that either Austria or France would take over Spain—with its possessions in Italy, The Netherlands, and the Americas—and thus dominate Europe. Alliances between different European countries were formed to support the two rival claimants to the throne and this led to what is called the War of the Spanish Succession. It lasted from 1702 until 1713 and involved all the major nations of Europe. It was the first major war fought to maintain what is known as a "**balance of power**" in which no single nation has more power than another.

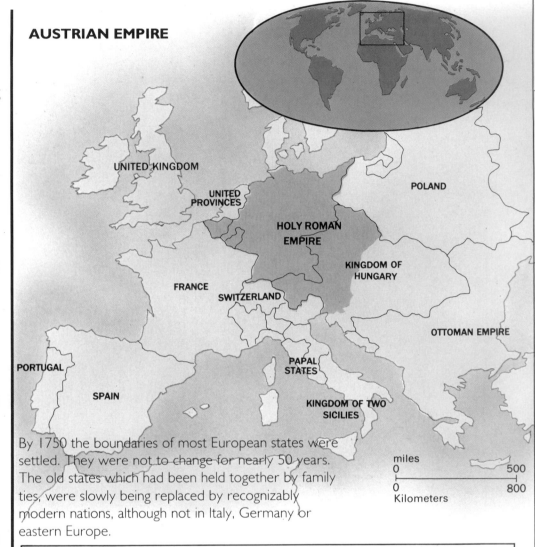

AUSTRIAN EMPIRE

By 1750 the boundaries of most European states were settled. They were not to change for nearly 50 years. The old states which had been held together by family ties, were slowly being replaced by recognizably modern nations, although not in Italy, Germany or eastern Europe.

miles
0   500
0   800
Kilometers

The English Revolution
There were many different causes of the English **Civil War**: its origins lay in the **authoritarian** behavior of the Stuart kings, who threatened the powers of the Parliament. Religious differences were important too: the Puritans in Parliament suspected the Stuart kings of Roman Catholic sympathies. Civil War broke out in 1642 and was resolved by the execution of King Charles the First in 1649.

For the next 11 years a **republic** was set up, the only one in British history, and the country was governed, first by Parliament and then by Oliver Cromwell (*above*), an army leader. After Cromwell's death in 1658 Charles the Second returned from exile and in 1660 was reinstated, but with his royal powers considerably reduced.

The Scientific Revolution

As a result of the Renaissance and Reformation, scientists began to question the idea that all knowledge came from the Roman Catholic Church. In mathematics, physics, astronomy and medicine new ideas were proposed, all of which could be quickly spread by the printing press. Scientists began to criticise existing theories and make their own observations.

The belief that the Earth was the centre of the Universe was challenged by Copernicus in 1543 and his ideas were supported by Galileo Galilei in the next century. Both men thought that the Sun was the centre of the Solar System, although few people believed them, but the explanation of how the Earth revolves daily on its axis around the Sun was not made until 1687, when Newton described the force of gravity that holds the Solar System together.

This explanation would not have been possible without the advances made in mathematics. New measuring instruments, such as the thermometer and the barometer, were invented. So too was the microscope, used by Robert Hooke to magnify animal and plant cells. In medicine, Vesalius showed the structure of the human body while William Harvey, who first discovered the circulation of blood, showed how the body worked.

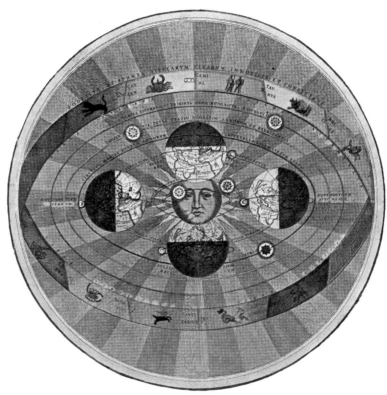

▲ The Solar System as described by Nicolaus Copernicus, a Polish scientist, in 1543. The Sun is shown at the centre of the Solar System with the Earth orbiting around it.

▼ Louis the Fourteenth visits the Académie Royale des Sciences in 1671. Founded in 1666, the French Académie was a learned body that helped spread new ideas.

▲ Isaac Newton, the scientist who explained the force of gravity. He also invented a reflecting telescope and introduced a branch of mathematics called calculus.

France, the absolute state

During the 1600s and 1700s much of Europe was ruled by kings, queens and emperors who were extremely powerful. Unlike European royal families today, these rulers were directly responsible for the economic, political and social lives of their countries and people.

Louis the Fourteenth, ruler of France from 1643 to 1715, was the most powerful of these **absolute monarchs**. All decisions were approved by him, and power was concentrated in his hands: he once summed up his position in the words 'L'état, c'est moi': *I am the state*. His absolute control was admired and copied by other European monarchs.

After a series of rebellions between 1648 and 1653 by leading nobles against the crown, France welcomed the strong rule of its king. But Louis required money for his many adventurous schemes. This was found by raising taxes and exploiting the wealth of France's colonies in Canada and the West Indies. The first great canal to be built in Europe since Roman times was constructed, while new roads and financial grants all helped to build up industry and commerce.

The wealth created was used to make the French army into the biggest in Europe and to finance the wars that Louis fought. After his death, however, further costly wars drained the country's resources and left France in a weakened conditioned.

▶ Under the rule of Louis the Fourteenth the borders of France were almost the same as they are today. They were made secure against attack from the Habsburgs who ruled Spain, Italy and the Holy Roman Empire. Inside France all opposition to Louis was crushed, and the king ruled from his palace at Versailles, near Paris.

◀ Louis the Fourteenth was the dominant ruler in Europe throughout the 1600s. He believed in Absolutism – that the king has complete control to rule his country as he wishes.

▼ At the salon of Madame Geoffrin in 1725. Groups of aristocrats met regularly to discuss art and philosophy. These salon meetings were the only places in which women could have any impact on the intellectual or political life of the day.

▼ The royal palace at Versailles was designed to glorify Louis the Fourteenth, the "Sun King." Surrounded by vast gardens and a park, the huge palace contained a Hall of Mirrors and many other sumptuously decorated state rooms. The high cost of running the palace was met by imposing taxes on the impoverished population.

▼ Plague, famine, and high taxes made many of the poor people homeless and they were forced to beg for food. The French peasants relied on the annual harvest—if the harvest failed they went hungry. Lack of food also made them more vulnerable to catching diseases such as the plague.

The Enlightenment

In almost every country in western Europe in the middle of the 1600s, an intellectual movement grew up, which became known as the Enlightenment. It questioned existing beliefs, and attempted to "throw light" on every area of human activity and thought. Its participants believed in the power of people to reason things out for themselves. Their thirst for knowledge included an interest in science and a curiosity about the peoples, plants, and animals from those parts of the world the Europeans were only just discovering for themselves.

One of the main achievements was the vast Encyclopedia (left) of all human knowledge, compiled between 1751 and 1777 by the French **philosopher**, Diderot. Another Frenchman, Descartes, provided the philosophical basis of the movement with the saying: "I think, therefore I am."

This new thinking challenged the existing authorities, such as the Church: some scientists, such as Galileo, were imprisoned, while the books of Descartes were banned. But this questioning of authority could not be supressed and in France was one of the causes of the **French Revolution**.

The emergence of Russia

Before 1450 much of southern Russia was controlled by the Khanate of the Golden Horde, a powerful state ruled by the Mongols of central Asia, who managed to isolate Russia from European developments. But as the power of the Mongols lessened, the small region of Muscovy exerted its independence. In 1480, its ruler, Ivan the Third, declared himself '**Tsar** of all the Russias' and appointed himself protector of the Orthodox Church.

Ivan the Third rebuilt Moscow with the help of Italian architects and began to expand the Muscovite state westwards. Expansion continued under successive tsars and by 1647 Russia dominated Siberia in the east but was unable to expand any farther towards Europe because of Polish and Swedish power.

In 1682 Peter the Great became Tsar of Russia and, until his death in 1725, he attempted to create a strong, **westernized** state. He toured western Europe in 1697–8 and on his return to Russia he introduced many reforms to modernize his country, giving it new industries and an improved education system. After a lengthy war with Sweden which ended in 1721, Russia gained control of the Baltic Sea. A new capital city – St Petersburg (Leningrad) – was built on the Baltic, which finally established Russia's presence in the West as a political power.

▲ The Palm Sunday parade in what is now Red Square in Moscow. The city clustered around the triangular fortress in the centre, called the Kremlin. St Basil's Cathedral (*on the left*) was built in the 1550s to celebrate the victories of Ivan the Fourth.

◄ Peter the Great in carpenter's dress. He travelled around Europe and learned shipbuilding techniques, which he later used to create a powerful Russian navy.

▼ Although the grand buildings of Russian cities were built of stone, the houses and churches of the Russian peasants were usually constructed with wooden logs.

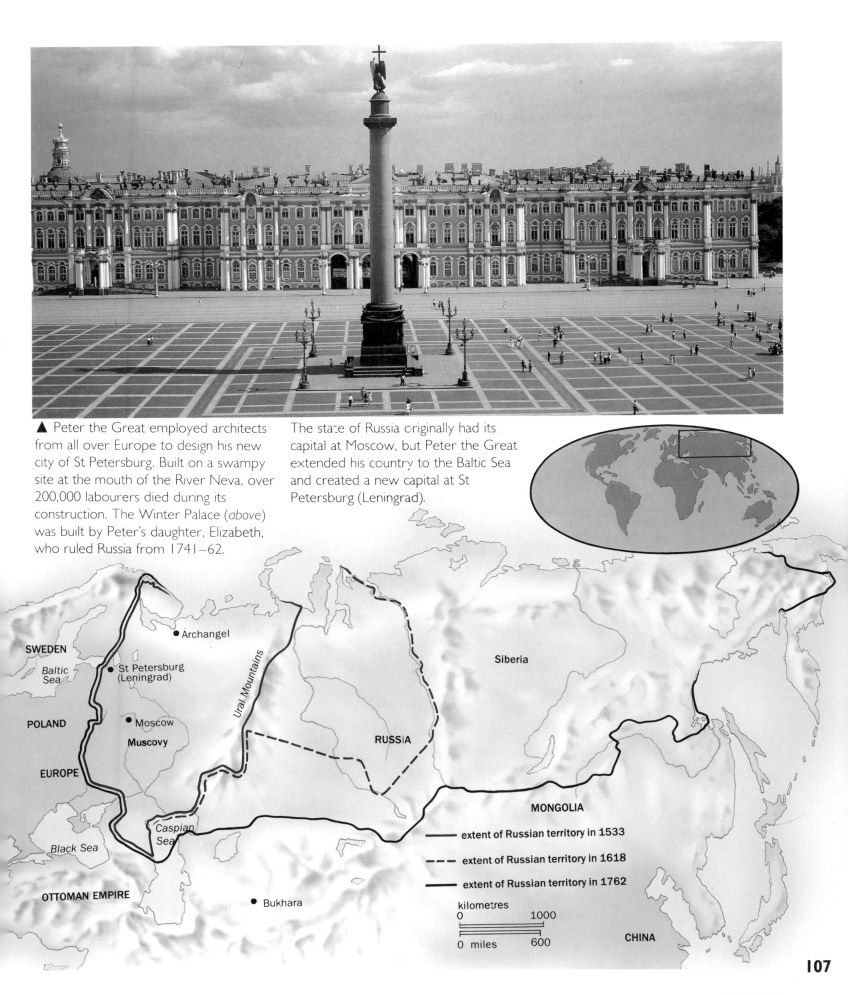

▲ Peter the Great employed architects from all over Europe to design his new city of St Petersburg. Built on a swampy site at the mouth of the River Neva, over 200,000 labourers died during its construction. The Winter Palace (*above*) was built by Peter's daughter, Elizabeth, who ruled Russia from 1741–62.

The state of Russia originally had its capital at Moscow, but Peter the Great extended his country to the Baltic Sea and created a new capital at St Petersburg (Leningrad).

SWEDEN

Baltic Sea

• Archangel

Ural Mountains

Siberia

• St Petersburg (Leningrad)

POLAND

• Moscow

Muscovy

RUSSIA

EUROPE

MONGOLIA

Caspian Sea

Black Sea

—— extent of Russian territory in 1533

- - - extent of Russian territory in 1618

—— extent of Russian territory in 1762

OTTOMAN EMPIRE

• Bukhara

kilometres
0   1000

0   miles   600

CHINA

107

China

From 1368 to 1644 the Ming Dynasty ruled China. At first the Ming emperors brought order and stability to the vast country whose growing population was twice that of all Europe. But harvest failures and high taxes caused discontent and weakened the Empire, which was also being threatened by attacks from Japan, and by the Manchus, a highly organized tribe from Manchuria in the northeast.

In 1644 the Manchus invaded China and seized power, setting up a new imperial dynasty—the Ch'ing Dynasty. They strengthened the state and expanded it north into Mongolia and west into Tibet and Sinkiang. Trading links were established with Europe, and China exported porcelain, silk, cotton, and tea. However, the Chinese imported only gold and silver from Europe and continued to develop their own culture, so that by 1750, China was wealthy, secure, and quite independent of Europe.

Japan

During the 1400s and 1500s Japan was torn apart by civil war. But in 1603 peace was restored when one of the many warlords—Ieyasu Tokugawa—became **shogun**, or military leader, under the Emperor. Like China, Japan developed independently of the outside world. From 1639, all Christian missionaries were expelled, trade with Europe all but stopped and the Japanese were forbidden to go abroad.

MANCHURIA
SINKIANG
Peking (Beijing)
Tientsin
Great Wall
KOREA
TIBET
Nanking
NEPAL
Canton
MACAO
TAIWAN
BURMA
SIAM   LAOS

Kilometers
0   500
0   300
miles

☐ extent of Ch'ing dynasty 1760

China was famous for its fine pottery. Some such as the Ming blue-and-white ware (right) was hand made at the imperial factory. More basic pots and vases were manufactured in numerous small workshops all over China. Some were produced for the home market. Others were exported to Europe. There they were highly prized for their fine design and were known as 'china'.

1648–1760

▲ Weaving silk on a loom. The Chinese silk industry was a vast enterprise, employing many thousands of workers, especially women, to produce silk textiles for home use and for export to Europe.

▲ Although the emperor ruled Japan in name, real military and administrative power lay with the shogun. The Shogun Ieyasu Tokugawa brought peace to Japan in 1603 and united the country under his family's rule until 1867.

▶ After 1639 the only port in Japan open to foreigners was at Nagasaki, where the Dutch, Chinese and Koreans were allowed to trade.

▼ The elaborate ritual of dressing a *samurai*. The *samurai* were the aristocratic warrior class in Japan famed for their bravery and devotion to the emperor. At one time they had the right to kill any commoner who offended them.

▲ Acupuncture – in which a number of fine needles are inserted into the skin to relieve pain and treat various ailments – has only recently been used in Western medicine, yet has been common practice in China for centuries.

109

Australia and New Zealand

By 1700 Europeans had penetrated every part of the world. They had established trading links across the Atlantic and Pacific Oceans and had completely disrupted **indigenous** societies in the Americas, south-east Asia and parts of Africa. Australia was the last 'unknown continent' that the Europeans invaded.

Both the Aborigines in Australia and the Maoris in New Zealand had developed thriving societies based on a **nomadic** existence of hunting and fishing which had remained undisturbed by any contact with the outside world. This traditional way of life came to an end with the arrival of the Europeans. In 1605 the Dutch explorer, Willem Janszoon, became the first European to arrive in Australia, and in 1642 Abel Tasman sailed right around Australia.

Australia remained undisturbed until 1768, when the British Admiralty sent Captain James Cook to explore the continent. He made three voyages in all, claiming Australia for the British crown in 1770, and exploring the whole of the western Pacific. In 1788 the first Europeans settled in Australia, **convicts** transported from Britain to serve their sentences. These colonists soon overcame the powerless Aborigines. In 1840 a British settlement was established in New Zealand and the Maoris were forced to accept the rule of the British crown.

▲ One of the crew from Captain Cook's ship, the *Endeavour*, barters with a Maori in New Zealand for a crayfish.

▲ When he reached Australia, Captain Cook found many birds, animals and plants previously unknown in Europe. One of the animals was the kangaroo.

The Dutchman, Abel Tasman, set out in 1642 to find the fabled southern continent. He sailed right around Australia, proving that it was an island, and also discovered Tasmania, named after him, and New Zealand which was named after the Dutch province of Zeeland.

▶ The Maoris came to New Zealand from the Pacific Islands in about AD800, traditionally in seven canoes. By the 1700s they numbered about 100,000 people. This European drawing shows the son of a Maori chief, Otegoongoon, with his face 'curiously tattooed'.

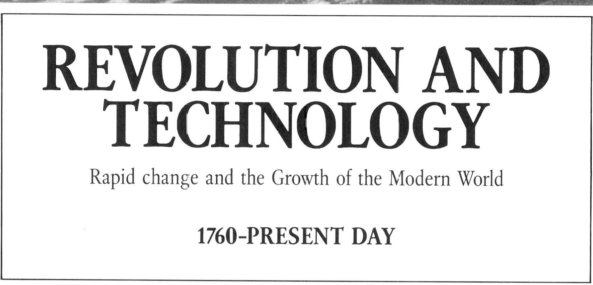

REVOLUTION AND TECHNOLOGY

Rapid change and the Growth of the Modern World

1760–PRESENT DAY

The World in 1760 and After

The world in 1760

In 1760 much of the world was dominated by Europe. Ever since the Genoese explorer Christopher Columbus had sailed across the Atlantic Ocean to the Caribbean in 1492, European merchants and sailors had been exploring the world. They had founded colonies and established trading links in every part of the world.

By 1760, Britain was the most powerful colonial and trading power in the world. Britain ruled large empires in North America and India. The British navy dominated the seas and Britain had established an extensive overseas trading network. France too was a wealthy and powerful **nation**, with colonies in the Caribbean. Spain and Portugal governed most of Central and South America, and, like the Netherlands, had colonies and trading posts in Africa and the Far East. In Asia, the Russians governed a huge empire that stretched from eastern Europe to the Pacific Ocean, while the Ottoman Turks ruled over much of eastern Europe, the Middle East and north Africa.

However, most of Africa and the wealthy empires of China and Japan remained independent of European control, although China and Japan had limited trade with Europe.

► In 1760 there were few parts of the world that were not under European control. North and South America, the coast of Africa, India and much of the Far East were governed from Europe and from them merchants sent back valuable cargoes to make Europe the wealthiest part of the world.

(*page 9, bottom left*) A British merchant ship known as an East Indiaman, in Calcutta, India.

(*page 9, bottom right*) Ambassadors at the Meridian Gate, Peking in China. There were four cities at Peking, each surrounded by great walls. China was only prepared to have limited trade with Europe.

The 13 Colonies

ATLAN

CARIBBEAN SEA

Spanish possessions

PACIFIC OCEAN

Portu posse

◄ In many parts of the world the European rulers enslaved the local population and made them work on sugar, tea and other plantations.

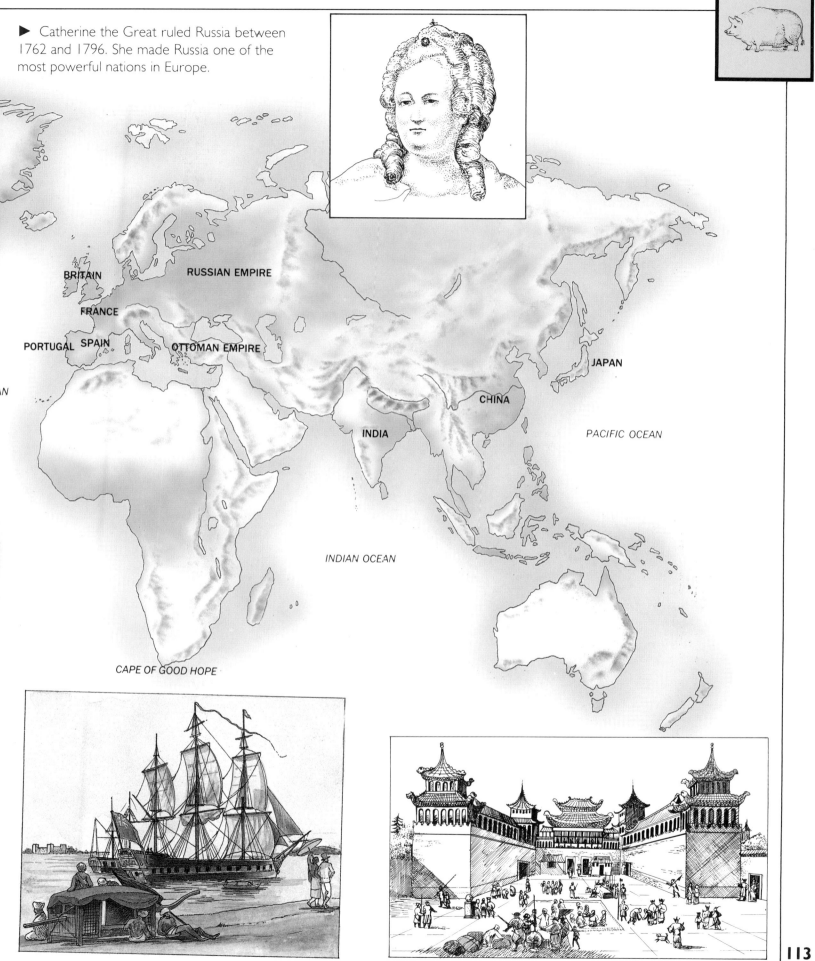

► Catherine the Great ruled Russia between 1762 and 1796. She made Russia one of the most powerful nations in Europe.

BRITAIN

RUSSIAN EMPIRE

FRANCE

PORTUGAL SPAIN

OTTOMAN EMPIRE

JAPAN

CHINA

INDIA

PACIFIC OCEAN

INDIAN OCEAN

CAPE OF GOOD HOPE

The Industrial Revolution

During the 1700s, Europe experienced a number of important social and economic changes whose effects remain today. The population of Europe doubled during the 1700s, and people began to move from the countryside to the cities. By 1800, Paris and London each contained more than one million inhabitants and other European cities were growing fast. To feed this rising population new agricultural techniques were developed.

The biggest changes took place in industry where Britain, followed by other countries, underwent what is known as the Industrial Revolution. Starting in Britain in about 1760, the Industrial Revolution transformed the way in which goods were produced. Machinery was developed that was powered by coal and water. Inventions such as the steam engine and steam pump, the blast furnace, and the spinning jenny revolutionized the manufacture of goods, particularly textiles. Methods of working changed too. Previously, most textiles had been produced in people's homes in 'cottage industries'. Now the new machines were built in factories where many workers – men, women and children – worked together under one roof.

As a result, British manufacturers could produce more goods than their foreign competitors. By 1815 Britain led world trade and was 'the workshop of the world'.

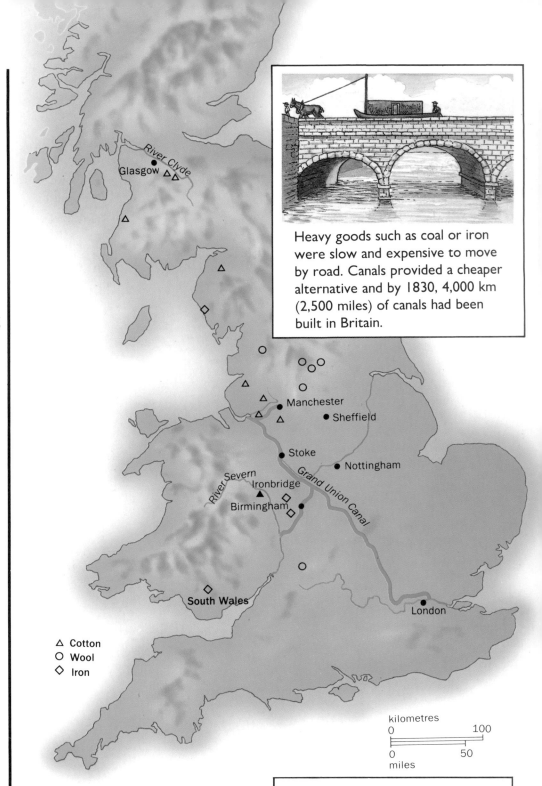

Heavy goods such as coal or iron were slow and expensive to move by road. Canals provided a cheaper alternative and by 1830, 4,000 km (2,500 miles) of canals had been built in Britain.

△ Cotton
○ Wool
◇ Iron

kilometres
0   100
0   50
miles

▲ After 1760, Britain became the industrial centre of the world. The country possessed plentiful supplies of coal and iron ore. A large network of roads, navigable rivers and canals was created to transport these raw materials to new industrial towns. There they were made into manufactured goods, notably textiles and ironware, and exported around the world.

The Agricultural Revolution

During the 1700s, Britain experienced an Agricultural Revolution. Farmers enclosed the old open, mixed fields of crops and pasture, and used new and intensive methods of farming. This increased food production but also drove farmworkers off the land and into the towns.

1760-1815

► Water power had been used for centuries to drive machines and so the first factories of the Industrial Revolution were all situated near a supply of running water, usually in hilly areas. After 1768, the development of the coal-fired steam engine meant that factories could be built wherever there was a good supply of coal.

▼ The British engineer, Thomas Newcomen, built the first steam engine in 1709 but it was only used for land drainage. In 1768, James Watt improved the original design and adapted it to drive factory machines.

▼ During the Agricultural Revolution, farmers began to experiment with new breeds of pig and other livestock. Larger pigs such as this Berkshire hog, and new breeds of sheep, produced twice as much meat as before. Improved cows led to an increase in dairy products.

◄ In 1764, James Hargreaves invented the spinning jenny – a machine that could spin up to 100 threads of cotton at one time. Previously, cotton was spun by hand, one thread at a time, by workers in their homes. The jenny replaced this domestic industry with workers who were employed in factories.

► The development of factories was seen as a threat to the jobs and independence of craftworkers. After 1810, a group of workers, known as Luddites, smashed machines in protest at their new working conditions This cartoon shows the Luddite leader disguised as a woman.

115

The American Revolution

Towards the end of the 1700s two revolutions occurred: the first in North America and the second in France. In both of them, people demanded democratic government and rights for the individual.

In 1763, Britain had defeated France to become the major colonial power in North America. But after the war, relations between Britain and its 13 colonies on the North Atlantic coast began to deteriorate. The immediate cause of these problems was taxation. The colonists made their own local laws but their finances and trade were controlled by the British government. Increasingly, the colonists resented paying taxes to a government in which they were not represented and which they did not elect or choose.

In 1774, the 13 states came together in a Continental Congress to discuss their relations with Britain. But revolution broke out in 1775 when shots were exchanged between colonists and the British army at Lexington. In 1776, Congress declared that the 13 colonies were **independent** of Britain, and by 1781 the American forces had defeated the British army. In 1783, the British recognized the independence of their former colonies. The rebels had won and they set up a new, united, nation – the United States of America. In 1789, George Washington became first president of the new nation.

▲ In 1774, a group of women colonists in Edenton, North Carolina protested against a British tax on tea by refusing to drink tea. The previous year, colonists in Boston threw £18,000 worth of tea into the harbour in a similar protest, now known as the Boston Tea Party.

▼ Signing the Declaration of Independence, issued in 1776 by the Continental Congress. Drawn up by Thomas Jefferson, the document declared that 'all men are created equal' and that they have the right to 'Life, Liberty and the Pursuit of Happiness'. Ideas such as these had a strong influence on later revolutionary movements.

The French Revolution

By 1789, French society was already deeply divided, for the middle classes resented the power of the king, the aristocracy and the Church. The people were heavily taxed, and many of them were starving. In 1789, King Louis XIV summoned the French parliament, to raise more taxes. Almost immediately, the **bourgeoisie**, the middle-class representatives, challenged the power of the king and set up a National Assembly to rule France. Riots broke out and the people of Paris stormed the royal fortress of the Bastille. The Revolution then quickly spread throughout the country. In 1792 the National Convention, which had replaced the Assembly, deposed the king and declared France a republic. Power passed to a political group known as the Girondins. In 1793 they executed the king for treason. Later the same year, a more radical group of politicians known as the Jacobins took power under Maximilien Robespierre. Their reign of terror lasted until 1794, during which they executed all those suspected of opposing the Revolution. In 1799 the Revolution ended when Napoleon Bonaparte seized power.

◄ The Tricolour, the new flag of Republican France.

Areas of resistance

FRANCE

Paris

Nantes

La Vendée

Bordeaux

Lyons

Marseilles

Place Louis XV (P de la Republic)

Tuileries Palace

River Seine

PARIS

Place de la Bastille

Place de la Nation

Guillotines erected

◄ The French Revolution began in Paris when the citizens stormed the Bastille Fortress in 1789. But it soon spread to the rest of the country. Some areas stayed loyal to the king; in the Vendée region of western France, a royalist revolt in 1793 was put down with considerable ferocity.

▼ Women led many of the marches and demonstrations during the French Revolution, demanding greater freedom and enough food to feed their families. Many suffered from starvation during the bad harvests. Despite their part in the Revolution, women were never allowed to vote or participate in the government.

▲ The guillotine quickly became the symbol of the Revolution. It was used to execute aristocrats and other opponents of the Revolution. More than 40,000 men and women were guillotined between 1789 and 1794.

Napoleonic Europe

The American colonies won their independence from Britain in 1783, with considerable French support. France had wanted revenge for the loss of its American colonies to Britain in 1763. But the American Revolution inspired people in France to seek their own freedom, and in 1789 a revolution broke out in France itself (page 13).

By 1793 all Europe was involved in the French Revolution. An alliance of European states was formed against France but France had an army of more than 750,000 – the biggest in Europe – and by 1797 France had defeated all its enemies except Britain. This success was due to the quality of the French commanders, particularly Napoleon Bonaparte, who, in 1796, at the age of 26, had taken command of the army. In 1799 he seized control of the French government and in 1804 he crowned himself Emperor of the French.

Napoleon reorganized the law, administration, education and economy of France. His army was unbeatable, and by 1812 he had conquered most of Europe. But his attempts to conquer Spain met with great resistance. In 1812 he unsuccessfully invaded Russia and his army suffered heavy losses retreating from Moscow. In 1815 Napoleon was finally defeated by the British and their allies at Waterloo. He was sent into exile on the South Atlantic island of St Helena, where he died in 1821.

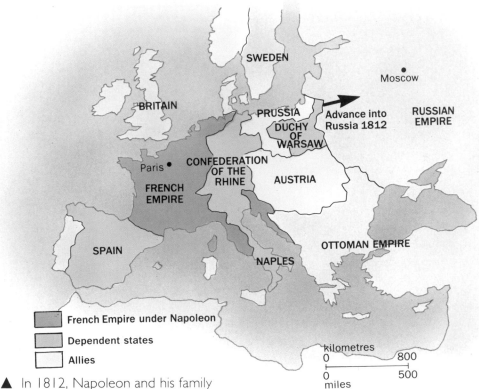

▲ In 1812, Napoleon and his family ruled an empire that dominated Europe. He reorganized Germany and Italy into allied states, and Prussia and Austria were considerably reduced in size and power. Only Britain remained independent. But the French Empire was weakened by the wars against Spain and Russia, and was finally overthrown in 1815.

► Napoleon was a military genius who had conquered most of Europe by 1812. His empire did not survive him, but many of his administrative and educational reforms are still in force in France today.

◄ A plate from a dinner service made for Napoleon. In 1798, Napoleon led a French army to Egypt to cut British trade links with India. While in Egypt, French archaeologists excavated the ancient Sphinx, which had been buried in the desert sand for hundreds of years and investigated the Pyramids.

◀ In 1808, Napoleon invaded Spain and placed his brother on the throne. Although the French introduced many reforms, their rule was not popular and the Spanish people revolted. Many civilians were killed, as this painting by Francisco Goya shows.

▼ The dates of independence of the European colonies in South America.

MEXICO
1821

CENTRAL AMERICAN
FEDERATION
1821-1838

VENEZUELA
1830

British, Dutch and French colonies
in GUYANA

COLUMBIA
1819

ECUADOR
1830

BRAZIL 1822

PERU
1821

BOLIVIA
1825

PARAGUAY
1811

CHILE
1818

URUGUAY 1828

ARGENTINA
1810

kilometres

0   1000

0   500
miles

▲ The French controlled the Caribbean island of Haiti, the richest colony in the world. Its wealth was created by the many slaves who worked on its plantations. In 1801, the slaves, led by Toussaint l'Ouverture, rose in revolt. L'Ouverture was captured and killed by the French in 1803, but in 1804 Haiti became an independent country.

▼ José de San Martin, (left) liberator of Argentina and Chile. He led his army across the Andes mountains, a military achievement.

▲ In 1808 Napoleon made his brother Joseph king of Spain. The Spanish colonies in South America refused to accept their new ruler and declared their independence. Led by Simon Bolívar (above) and José de San Martin, all the former Spanish territories became independent by 1825.

119

The Impact of Revolution

Industrial nations

The upheavals caused by the Industrial and French Revolutions affected every aspect of social and political life for the next 100 years.

Although the Industrial Revolution began in Britain, the new **technologies** and methods of production soon spread to Belgium, France, Germany and Italy. At first, Britain was strong enough to fight off any competition. In 1850, one-quarter of all the world's trade passed through British ports and over one-third of the world's industrial output was British. The first railway was tested in the north of England in 1825 and the first passenger train operated between Liverpool and Manchester in 1830. The railway revolutionized communications, and by 1870 there were 25,000 km (15,500 miles) of railway track in Britain alone.

Other countries soon began to challenge British industrial and economic supremacy. After 1870, new steel and chemical industries were established in Germany, while by 1900 the United States had become the most powerful industrial nation in the world, with vast steel, oil and food production industries. Russia, too, developed an iron and steel industry and Japan started to build up an industrial economy.

○ Coalfields
◇ Iron ore fields
□ Textile industry

▲ The Industrial Revolution began in Britain but soon spread throughout Europe. Mines and factories opened up near supplies of coal and iron and new towns were built to accommodate the expanding workforce. Across Europe, the population increased dramatically as the new factories required more workers.

▶ Men, women and children worked long hours for low pay in the mines and factories of industrial Britain. In the early coal mines men hacked the coal out of the seams and women then dragged it or carried it along the narrow tunnels. From the 1830s, however, laws were introduced to improve working conditions.

1815–1880

▲ Until the 1850s, steel was expensive to produce, costing almost 20 times as much as iron. In 1856, Henry Bessemer, an English engineer, developed a cheap way of producing steel and within a few years steel had replaced iron in the construction of railways, ships, machinery and buildings. This factory, in the Ruhr valley in West Germany, made weapons from steel.

◄ In 1851, Britain held an international exhibition in London to show off the industrial and manufacturing might of the country. The Great Exhibition was housed in a remarkable iron and glass building, called the Crystal Palace; it was erected in only seven months.

▲ The Industrial Revolution created many new towns and enlarged many old ones, but conditions in the towns were overcrowded and poor. Many of the houses were badly built and had no running water or sewage disposal and they quickly became slums. Disease and poverty were common in all major cities.

► Poor children were sent to work in factories or even mines as soon as they were old enough to walk and talk. They received little formal education and were made to work long hours for little pay. Child labour was common in European and American factories until well into the 20th century.

Europe after 1815

After Napoleon's defeat in 1815, the victorious allies met in Vienna to redraw the map of Europe. The French monarchy was restored, and Austria became dominant in central Europe. Throughout Europe, aristocratic government was restored and Napoleon's reforms were reversed everywhere except in France.

The Vienna settlement lasted only a few years. The French Revolution had introduced to Europe two ideas: democracy, in which the people had a say in the government and **nationalism**, in which people speaking a common language and living together in one country or region had the right to rule themselves. However, the 1815 settlement left many peoples under undemocratic, foreign control, and major uprisings soon occurred. In 1821, the Greeks revolted against their Turkish rulers and won independence in 1829, and in 1830 the Belgians overthrew Dutch rule.

In 1848 revolutions occurred throughout Europe. The monarchy was again overthrown in France and nationalists revolted against Austrian rule in Italy, Germany and Hungary. By 1851 the revolts had been crushed. But nationalism remained strong in Italy and Germany. Led by Count Cavour, the various Italian states drove out the Austrians by 1866 and Italy was united by 1870. In 1871, all Germany was united under the powerful rule of Prussia.

▲ In Britain, the Chartists — a mass movement of men and women — demanded political reform and the right to vote. Between 1838 and 1848 they held vast demonstrations and presented a series of petitions to Parliament.

▶ In 1848, the German thinker Karl Marx wrote the *Communist Manifesto* urging workers to overthrow undemocratic governments. At the time, the book was not widely read, but during the 20th century, Marx's ideas have strongly influenced modern revolutionary movements in Russia, China and South America.

▼ In 1848, many countries in Europe erupted in revolution.

- Centres of revolution in 1848
— GERMAN CONFEDERATION

Berlin
PRUSSIA • Warsaw
Frankfurt
Paris • Prague
Vienna • Budapest
FRANCE AUSTRIAN EMPIRE
Milan
Venice
ITALIAN STATES OTTOMAN EMPIRE
Rome

RUSSIAN EMPIRE

kilometres
0   400
0   200
miles

1815-1880

Science

▲ This contemporary cartoon attacks the British biologist Charles Darwin, who, in 1859, published *The Origin of Species*. In this book he proposed that over many thousands of years humans had evolved from apes.

▼ In 1861 the French chemist Louis Pasteur discovered that diseases do not occur by themselves but are the result of germs carried in the air. This discovery led him to develop pasteurization, a method of sterilizing (cleaning) milk.

▲ A picture taken during the American Civil War, the first war to be recorded by photograph. In 1839, the Frenchman Louis Daguerre produced the first successful photograph. Only one photograph could be produced at a time.

During the 1800s, science and medicine were revolutionized, as a series of remarkable developments transformed the way in which people lived and thought about the world around them. Scientists such as Louis Pasteur discovered the cause of diseases; doctors such as Joseph Lister introduced effective antiseptics for the prevention of infections; and, for the first time, the workings of the human mind were scientifically investigated when the Austrian doctor, Sigmund Freud, began his investigations into mental illness at the end of the century. In 1859, the British biologist Charles Darwin shocked the Western world when he suggested that human life had begun, not with their creation by God, but through a long process of evolution from the apes. Throughout the 1800s, there was a constant stream of new technological developments.

▲ In the 1890s, the Frenchwoman Marie Curie investigated uranium, which is now used to produce nuclear power.

▲ In the late 1800s and early 1900s, Sigmund Freud studied human behaviour by interpreting dreams.

The growth of the United States

When the United States of America became independent from Britain in 1783, it consisted of only the 13 original British colonies on the Atlantic east coast. But it grew quickly after independence, and in little more than 80 years had trebled in size, reaching right across to the Pacific Ocean, and up to the Arctic Circle in the north.

In 1803, France sold the land to the west of the Mississippi River for $15 million, which doubled the size of the country. By 1867, gains from Spain, Britain, Mexico and Russia gave the country its present shape. But throughout the 1800s there were fierce battles for control between the European settlers and the native Americans, or American Indians, who had lived there for thousands of years. Though brave, the American Indians had little defence against American troops, and by 1890 the Indians had been overcome and confined to reservations.

Between 1803 and 1900, the population of the United States rose from four million to 90 million. Many of these people were immigrants fleeing from poverty and oppression in Europe. They spoke many different languages and brought many skills to their new country. Some prospered, others remained poor, but a rich and strong nation emerged. By 1900, the United States was the world's most powerful industrial and commercial nation.

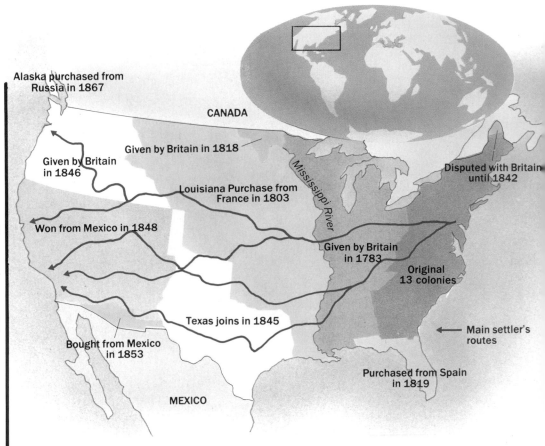

▲ By 1848, the original 13 American colonies on the Atlantic coast had expanded across the continent to the Pacific Ocean. It was many years later before these vast tracts of land were fully settled by farmers and their families, who moved slowly westwards from the crowded eastern states.

▼ In 1828 the first railway line was opened in America and by 1869 the two sides of the continent were connected by 85,000 km (52,000 miles) of railway. The railway did much to open up the West and to create a truly united country.

► The early North American settlers lived hard lives. They had to defend their lands against the local Indians and they were always at the mercy of bad weather or harvest failure. The settlers built homes of turf or even soil and it was years before they could afford to build secure wooden houses.

▼ In 1861, civil war broke out in America between the southern states, who wished to keep slaves on their plantations, and the northern states, who wished to abolish **slavery**. The northern states won the war with great brutality in 1865, but the south was devastated. This picture shows a New York ferry, converted into a gunboat for use by the northern states.

► Sitting Bull was chief of the Sioux tribe and one of the most famous of Indian leaders. In 1876 he killed General Custer at the Battle of the Little Big Horn and continued to fight for the rights of the Indian peoples until his death in 1890.

► Harriet Tubman was an escaped slave who spent much of her life fighting slavery. During the Civil War she organized an escape network known as the Underground Railway, through which more than 300 slaves escaped to freedom.

125

Imperialism and Empire

Empire-builders

In 1880, most of Africa consisted of independent nations. Their economies were based on agriculture, and they traded with other African countries. Contact with Europe was limited, although the British, French and Portuguese maintained small colonial trading posts on the coast, while the Ottoman Empire had loose control of north-eastern Africa. By 1914, with the exception of the independent states of Ethiopia and Liberia, every part of Africa was controlled by Europeans. Africa's economy had been transformed to provide raw materials for European industries.

Similarly the British had established complete control of India and its neighbours, and of Australia and New Zealand, while much of the Far East was ruled by other European powers. The main reason for this expansion overseas was that, by 1880, the Industrial Revolution had spread across Europe. The new industries needed cheap supplies of raw materials, and this led European nations to exploit the vast and untapped resources of Africa and the Far East. By 1914 Britain had built up the world's biggest empire. It covered one-quarter of the world's land surface and included one-quarter of its population. France, Belgium,

1880

Portuguese
British
French

1914

LIBERIA

ETHIOPIA

Spanish
German
Italian
Belgian
Independent

▲ In 1880, most of Africa consisted of independent nations, with only the Ottoman Empire ruling any significant territory in Africa. By 1914, the continent had been carved up by Europeans and only two nations remained independent of foreign control.

▲ The Englishwoman Mary Kingsley was an enterprising explorer who travelled throughout West Africa in the late 1800s. Many of the people she encountered had never met a European woman before.

▼ Cecil Rhodes was Prime Minister of the British-controlled Cape Colony in South Africa. He dreamed of building a railway from the Cape in the south to Cairo in the north that would run entirely through British territory.

▲ In 1869, the Suez Canal was opened connecting the Mediterranean Sea to the Indian Ocean. Because of its strategic position on the route from Britain to its empire in India, it was acquired by Britain in 1875.

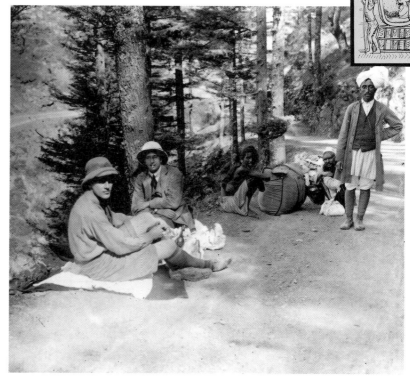

▲ British influence in India was considerable. Many of the British people living in India preserved as much as possible their British customs and ways of life. Here two Englishmen take afternoon tea, attended by their Indian servants.

European Settlement of South Africa

The first European settlers in South Africa were the Dutch, who established a colony on the Cape of Good Hope in 1652. The British took over the colony in 1814 and in 1833 abolished the slavery of black Africans on the farms and plantations. This angered the Boers, as the original Dutch settlers were known, and in 1835 they trekked inland to form two new independent republics. Continual conflicts between the Boers and the British led to war in 1899. By 1902 the British had won, and in 1910 the country was united and became an independent state known as the Union of South Africa.

▼ Southern Africa is rich in gold and diamonds. During the late 1800s a number of powerful mining companies were set up, controlled by Europeans and using slave labour.

127

Portugal, Spain, Italy and the newly-united Germany all established colonies in Africa. Meanwhile the United States acquired territory in the Caribbean and the Far East. By 1914 the United States and eight European nations controlled eighty-five per cent of the world's land surface.

China and Japan

Until the mid-1800s, very few Europeans had been allowed into the empires of China or Japan. The Chinese in particular had a hatred of foreigners and allowed them to trade only in certain areas. Britain, however, was keen to extend its influence. In 1839, it went to war with China, and in 1842 the Chinese were forced to sign a treaty surrendering Hong Kong and allowing Britain to trade in other ports. Within China, revolts against the Ch'in Dynasty weakened the empire, allowing European influence to increase. The Chinese government's failure to resist the Europeans in turn led to further rebellions and in 1911 a revolution finally over-threw the empire and established a republic.

Japan had almost no trading contact with foreigners until 1853, when an American naval squadron sailed to Japan and forced the Japanese to trade with the United States. Europeans followed and Japan made trade agreements with many countries. Over the years, Japan developed railways and factories and by 1905 had become a major industrial nation.

▲ By 1905 Britain, France and Russia dominated much of China and Japan had gained an empire of its own in Korea and Taiwan.

► In 1900 a Chinese secret society known as the 'Boxers' rebelled against Western intervention, attacking railways, factories and European embassies. The rebellion was put down by European and Japanese armies, who established control over much of the country. This Chinese cartoon attacks Westerners.

▼ In the 1850s the waterfront of the Chinese city of Canton was full of Europeans but they were not allowed into the interior of China for many years.

▲ In 1853 and 1854 the American naval commander Matthew Perry visited Japan and forced the government to grant trading concessions to American shipping. It was the first Japanese contact with foreigners for more than 200 years.

▲ In 1872 the first railway line was completed in Japan by British engineers. Within 30 years, more than 8000 km (5000 miles) of track had been laid and Japan had become one of the most powerful industrial states in the world.

▼ In their rush to modernize their country, many Japanese people, including the royal family, gave up their traditional costumes in favour of Western clothes.

A changing world

In the years immediately after 1900 wars broke out in Europe, Africa and the Far East, and there was internal unrest in many industrial nations. Much of the trouble was caused by the fact that the European powers were competing against each other to control trade and to increase their empires. By 1900 Germany had become the major industrial power in Europe, and this led to considerable rivalry with the established industrial nations such as Britain. An **arms race** developed between the European powers. Britain, France and Russia formed an alliance to protect themselves against Germany, while Germany allied itself with Austria.

There was also considerable social unrest in many countries. In 1905 revolution broke out in Russia against the autocratic rule of the Tsar. Although unsuccessful, the revolution seriously weakened the country. In 1912 war broke out in eastern Europe as the local peoples fought to overthrow their Turkish rulers and prevent Austria from taking over. This fighting increased tension throughout Europe, which found itself divided into two heavily armed camps. In Ireland there was almost civil war by 1914, caused by the demands of the Irish for self-government, while throughout Europe poor wages and bad working conditions led to much social unrest. By 1914 the whole continent was in turmoil.

SHE. IT IS TIME I GOT OUT OF THIS PLACE. WHERE SHALL I FIND THE KEY?

CONVICTS AND LUNATICS HAVE NO VOTE FOR PARLIAMENT

Should all Women be classed with these?

◄ Elected parliaments were the most common form of government in Europe and the United States. By 1900 working men had gained the vote in most countries but women were not allowed to vote at all, except in New Zealand, which in 1893 became the first country to give women the vote. The United States followed in 1920, but it was not until 1928, after many years of struggle, that all British women over 21 were allowed to vote.

▼ A dole queue in Britain. During the late 1800s governments began to take responsibility for the welfare of their people. Many countries introduced compulsory education, and pensions were provided for the old. State insurance was introduced to protect workers against unemployment or sickness and workers received 'dole' money if they lost their jobs.

▼ In the years leading up to 1914 there was an arms race in Europe between the major powers. Weapons such as this German howitzer were capable of great destruction.

Transport

Throughout the 1800s new forms of transport revolutionized communications throughout the world. Railways, steamships, motor cars, bicycles and, in the early years of the 1900s, airships and aircraft, all increased the speed and efficiency of human travel. An organized tourist industry started to grow up, and people began to visit foreign countries in large numbers. Trade between different countries became easier and cheaper, while refrigeration enabled perishable foodstuffs to be transported around the world. As a result of these developments all parts of the world were linked together as never before.

▼ The development of the bicycle in the mid-1800s offered a cheap form of transport and recreation to large numbers of people.

▲ The Zeppelin airship was built in Germany in 1920 and was originally for military purposes.

◄ In 1907 an American, Henry Ford, started mass production of his Model T motor car.

▼ The first controlled flight was made by the Wright brothers in 1903.

▼ Railways gave poor people the chance to travel for the first time in their lives.

▼ In 1882 the refrigerator ship *Dunedin* brought frozen meat from New Zealand to Europe.

The World at War

The First World War

In 1914 war broke out in Europe, lasting for four years and involving the whole world. The immediate cause of the war was the assassination of the heir to the Austrian throne in June 1914. Austria blamed its neighbour and enemy Serbia for the murder and declared war on it; soon all Europe was at war. Few nations remained **neutral** and fighting extended overseas for control of Germany's African and Far Eastern colonies, and for Turkish territories in the Middle East.

Between France and Germany a line of defensive trenches stretched along the Western Front, where millions of soldiers were killed. In eastern Europe, the war was equally savage. For three years there was stalemate, but in 1917 the Russian Revolution forced Russia to leave the war. In an effort to starve Britain and France into surrender, Germany attacked their supply ships in the Atlantic. Some American ships were sunk, and in 1917 the United States declared war on Germany. The vast numbers of American troops proved decisive, and in November 1918 the war ended. Of the 65 million men who fought in the war 10 million died, and more than 20 million were injured. It was the bloodiest war in human history.

▲ Most soldiers in the First World War spent their time in damp and dangerous trenches on the Western Front, being bombarded by enemy shells.

▶ For the first time in history, whole populations were involved in war. Many women worked, producing armaments and keeping industry going while the men were in the army.

▼ The First World War split Europe into two armed camps.

BRITAIN

GERMANY

RUSSIA

FRANCE

AUSTRIA-HUNGARY

ROMANIA

SERBIA

BULGARIA

ITALY

OTTOMAN EMPIRE

GREECE

Allied Powers

Central Powers

Western Front

kilometres
0   800
0   500
miles

The Russian Revolution

In 1917 a revolution took place in Russia that was to change the course of modern history. The revolution occurred because many people suffered poverty and hardship. The government of Nicholas the Second was brutal but inefficient and it fought the war against Germany very incompetently.

In February 1917 a **general strike** broke out in Petrograd (as St Petersburg was then known; today the city is called Leningrad) in protest against the conduct of the war and the economic chaos at home. The army joined the strike and Nicholas was forced to abdicate his throne. A provisional government was formed but it had little support and in October 1917 the Communists (or Bolsheviks, as they were known) seized power. Led by

Vladimir Ilyich Illyanov (Lenin)

Lenin (*left*), the Bolsheviks quickly took control of the country and declared a Soviet republic, known today as the Soviet Union. The Bolsheviks made peace with Germany. The large estates were broken up and given to the peasants, banks were taken into state control and workers were given control of their factories. The world's first communist state had been founded.

▶ In 1924 Joseph Stalin succeeded Lenin as head of the Soviet Union. He took all the land into state ownership and forced the peasants to work on the new collective farms. This is a poster advertising collectivism.

◀ Alexandra Kollontai was the only woman in the Bolshevik government. She was committed to economic change and to equality between women and men.

▲ Four-fifths of the Russian population were peasants. Some of them found work hauling barges down the River Volga.

The aftermath of war

In 1919, the 30 states involved in the First World War met at Versailles in France, to draw up a peace settlement. Four empires – Germany, Austria, Russia and Turkey – had collapsed and many countries wanted independence. The map of Europe was redrawn and some new countries came into existence. The League of Nations was set up to work for peaceful settlements rather than war, but few countries obeyed its instructions.

The Versailles settlement was soon in trouble. The German economy collapsed because of the reparations (payments) Germany was forced to make for its part in the war. Other nations suffered from the heavy repayments they had to make to the United States for money borrowed during the war. The result was considerable political and economic upheaval. In 1929, an economic crisis, known as the Great Depression began.

Millions of people were thrown out of work. During the 1930s there was widespread unemployment and social unrest in Europe and in the United States. The president of the United States, Franklin Roosevelt helped the poor and unemployed through a programme of government aid known as the New Deal. In Germany, however, an extreme nationalist, Adolf Hitler, came to power in 1933. He promised to set unemployed Germans to work by restoring German power in Europe.

► The Treaty of Versailles in 1919 broke up the German, Austrian and Russian empires and replaced them with new states throughout Eastern Europe. Germany became smaller and was split into two parts. Poland and Finland re-emerged as independent nations. The Austro–Hungarian Empire was split into four new countries, with parts of it also going to Italy, Poland and Romania. Three new states were created on the Baltic.

◄ During the early 1900s, the first films appeared. They were in black and white and had no sound. By 1930, films were in colour and had sound. Many films were produced in Hollywood, California, known as the film capital of the world.

▼ In 1929, the value of shares on the American Stock Exchange on Wall Street crashed as investors lost confidence in the American economy. Banks failed and an economic depression began that soon spread throughout the world.

134

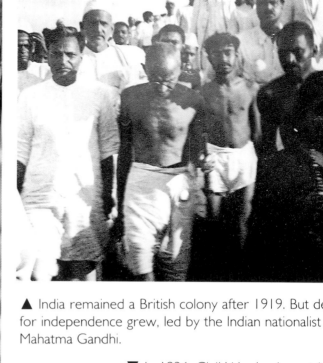

▲ India remained a British colony after 1919. But demands for independence grew, led by the Indian nationalist Mahatma Gandhi.

▲ The Depression caused terrible suffering to American farmers. Prices fell and drought affected the crops. Whole families were forced to leave their farms in the mid-west to look for other work in California.

▼ **Fascism** was carried to extremes by Adolf Hitler, leader of the Nazi party, shown below. In 1933 Hitler was named German Chancellor. Under his dictatorship, economic, cultural and religious life were all brought under central government control.

▼ In 1936, Civil War broke out in Spain between the Republican Government and the Fascists led by General Franco. Helped by Italy and Germany, Franco defeated the government in a brutal war. He ruled Spain as **dictator** from 1939 to 1975. This poster shows a soldier off to fight against the Fascists saying to his baby: 'I Go to Fight for Your Future'.

The Second World War

When Hitler became the leader of Germany in 1933, he created a German empire in Central Europe. By 1939 he had seized Austria and Czechoslovakia. Most European nations were anxious to avoid the horrors of another war, but when in 1939 Hitler invaded Poland, Britain and France declared war on Germany. Italy joined the war on the German side.

For six years, war raged in Europe, North Africa, Russia and the Pacific. Continual air raids destroyed many cities. By 1941, Germany had conquered most of Europe, except for Britain, and had advanced into Russia. In the Far East, Japan allied with Germany and invaded China, Burma and other parts of South East Asia.

In December 1941, Japanese planes bombed the American naval base at Pearl Harbor, in Hawaii. The United States sided with Britain and together they reconquered North Africa, invaded Italy, and, in 1944, liberated France from German control. As American and British troops advanced on Germany from the west, Russian troops advanced from the east. As they neared Berlin in April 1945, Hitler committed suicide and the war in Europe ended. In August the Americans dropped the first atomic bomb on the Japanese city of Hiroshima and a second on Nagasaki, and Japan surrendered.

It was a brutal end to a brutal war. Fifty million people had been killed or injured and another 43 million wounded. Europe was devastated.

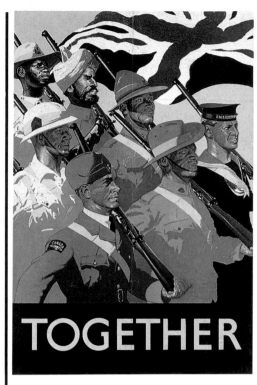

▲ War touched every part of the globe as soldiers from all over the British Empire fought the war on Britain's side.

▲ One of Hitler's most dreadful aims was to destroy the entire Jewish population of Europe. More than six million Jews and other peoples died in concentration camps such as this one at Buchenwald.

▼ In 1942, the German conquest of Europe reached its greatest extent. Very few countries managed to avoid the fighting.

USA joined the war in 1941

Japan invaded China in 1937 and declared war on USA in 1941

Neutral countries

German domination at its greatest extent in 1942

▲ On 6 August 1945, an atomic bomb was dropped on the Japanese city of Hiroshima. This photograph shows the terrible devastation caused by the bomb.

◀ In 1945, the American, Russian and British leaders – Franklin Roosevelt, Joseph Stalin and Winston Churchill – met at Yalta in Russia to decide how to divide up post-war Europe.

▼ After 1945, the German capital Berlin, like Germany itself, was divided into two. Conflicts arose and in 1961 the Berlin Wall was built to divide east Berlin from west. In 1989, after popular protest, the wall was dismantled, and in 1990 Germany was reunited.

▲ In 1947, India gained independence from Britain. India became mainly Hindu, and a new State, Pakistan, was created for the Muslims. Both Burma and Ceylon (Sri Lanka) also received their freedom. There was considerable bloodshed during this partition, and the Indian leader Gandhi was assassinated.

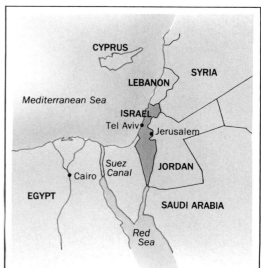

In 1948, a Jewish homeland was created in Israel. The Palestinian occupants of the country were defeated by the new Israeli army. Since then, three more wars have broken out between Israel and its Arab neighbours.

A Troubled World

The Cold War

In 1945 American troops liberated Western Europe from German control, while Russian troops had liberated Eastern Europe. Together the **superpowers** of the Soviet Union and the United States dominated Europe. But differences soon emerged between them. The Soviet Union felt threatened by the American presence in Europe, while the United States feared that the Soviet Union wanted to extend its control of Eastern Europe. By 1949, Europe was divided into two armed camps, both engaged in what was known as the Cold War.

When war broke out in Korea in 1950 and then in Vietnam in 1954, the Soviet Union and China supported one side while the United States supported the other. In other disputes too, in the Middle East, Africa and South America, the two superpowers supported opposing sides. The years from 1945 were also marked by an increasing nuclear arms race between the superpowers.

In 1985 Mikhail Gorbachev became Soviet premier and introduced a new policy of *glasnost* (openness) and *perestroika* (economic reform) in the Soviet Union. Rivalry between the two powers began to decrease as both the United States and the Soviet Union discussed the possibility of

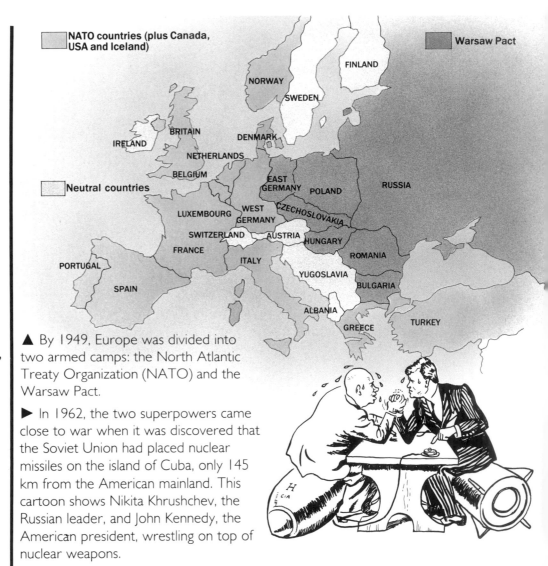

▲ By 1949, Europe was divided into two armed camps: the North Atlantic Treaty Organization (NATO) and the Warsaw Pact.

▶ In 1962, the two superpowers came close to war when it was discovered that the Soviet Union had placed nuclear missiles on the island of Cuba, only 145 km from the American mainland. This cartoon shows Nikita Khrushchev, the Russian leader, and John Kennedy, the American president, wrestling on top of nuclear weapons.

◀ In 1968 Soviet troops invaded Prague, when Czechoslovakia tried to break away from Soviet control. But by 1989 Soviet control had relaxed and popular pro-democracy movements swept through Czechoslovakia, Hungary, Romania and the rest of Eastern Europe.

◀ Superpower rivalry extended into outer space. In 1957, the Soviet Union launched the world's first satellite into orbit around the world. In 1961 the Soviet Union became the first country to put a man into space. The United States launched a series of rockets with the aim of landing people on the moon. This they achieved in 1969. In 1975, however, both countries worked together on a joint space mission.

▶ In 1969, the American astronaut Neil Armstrong (right) became the first person to land on the moon. For the first time in human history, it was possible to see our planet Earth from space (far right).

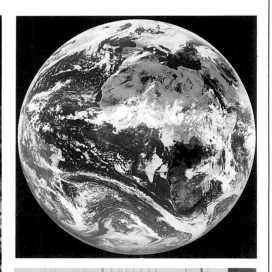

▼ Vietnamese refugees run to a helicopter to take them to safety. Between 1954 and 1975, war raged between North and South Vietnam. The Soviet Union and China supported the North, and the United States supported the South. The war cost many American and Vietnamese lives, and ended with victory for the North after America withdrew its troops in 1973.

▲ In 1987 Ronald Reagan, the American president, and Mikhail Gorbachev, the Soviet leader, signed a treaty to dismantle intermediate-range nuclear missiles. This decision was welcomed by many people who hoped that the treaty marked the first step towards complete nuclear disarmament.

139

nuclear disarmament. In 1989 popular uprisings in Eastern Europe also eased tension and heralded the ending of the Cold War.

China

In 1911, China became a republic after a revolt by the Kuomintang political party overthrew the Manchu emperor. However, real power did not lie with the new government but with powerful **warlords**, who ruled the many provinces of China. In 1926, the Kuomintang general, Chiang Kai-shek defeated the warlords with the help of the Chinese Communist Party. He set up a national government in the city of Nanking. Once in power, he threw the Communists out of the government and killed many of their leaders. Fighting broke out between the two sides. By 1949, the Communists, led by Mao Ze-dong, were triumphant.

The Communists under Mao set about rebuilding China. They put industry and agriculture under state control and made huge attempts to feed the 1,000 million people in the country. China allied itself with the Soviet Union and received technical aid in developing the country. But in 1960 the two governments quarrelled and the aid stopped. Since then, the Communist Party has kept the country under tight control. Dissent against the government was squashed during the Cultural Revolution 1966-1969.

◀ In October 1934, the Communists decided to leave their stronghold on the coast of China and move inland. Led by Mao Ze-dong, 100,000 people set out on the Long March. They covered 60 to 100 kilometres a day and arrived at their destination a year later. Only 30,000 of the original marchers completed the 10,000-kilometre march.

▲ In order to unite the country, the Chinese leader Mao Ze-dong encouraged a cult of personality. Millions of people bought and read *The Thoughts of Chairman Mao*, his collection of sayings.

▶ In 1989, students in Beijing (Peking) and other cities requested more democracy and freedom in China. The Chinese government refused to grant these requests, and crushed the peaceful student movement with military force. Many people were killed or imprisoned.

Technology and Pop Culture

Today the regions of our world are more closely linked than ever before. It is possible to travel around the globe in hours, while satellites can broadcast events and relay messages around the globe in seconds. Television has brought every area of the world into our homes and there are few places in the world left undisturbed by tourists. As a result, differences between the various countries of the world are slowly breaking down. Computers speak their own common language to each other across the globe. Fashions in clothes, music, design and art are now universal.

▲ The first satellite was launched by the Soviet Union in 1957. Since then, thousands of satellites have been sent into orbit around the Earth.

◀ Satellite communication has brought television to the remotest parts of the world.

Pop music started in the 1950s. Groups such as the Beatles (*left*) and singers like Michael Jackson (*right*) are known in every country. Their records sell millions of copies.

A divided world

Since 1945 a wide gap has emerged between the rich countries of Europe, North America, Australasia and the Far East, and the poorer countries of Africa, Asia and Central and South America.

The rich countries all have highly-developed industries and economies. In Western Europe, 12 countries have joined together in a Common Market to bring their economies closer together, while in the Far East, Japan has become the richest nation in the world. In contrast, many of the poor countries have little industry and only primitive agriculture. Many of these countries only received their independence in the 1960s and 1970s when the European powers such as France and Britain began to dismantle their overseas empires. In countries such as Tanzania and Zambia, this move to independence was peaceful, but in Algeria and Mozambique, for example, there was much bloodshed. Some of these new nations are prosperous but many suffer considerable poverty made worse by famine, civil war, disease and over-population.

In order to build up their economies, many poor nations have borrowed money from the rich nations of Europe and the United States. The repayment of these loans has been expensive and has kept many of the poor nations in poverty. Today the gap between rich and poor is one of the world's most urgent problems.

▲ The conflict between Israel and its Arab neighbours has made the Middle East one of the world's most troubled areas.

◀ In 1910, South Africa became an independent nation. Since then the white minority of the population has held absolute power through a system called **apartheid** (racial segregation). Apartheid denies all rights to the majority of South Africans, who are black. Despite repression, black resistance continues. In 1990 the ban against political opposition groups was lifted and some political prisoners, such as Nelson Mandela of the African National Congress (ANC) were freed after many years in prison.

▼ In 1979, Ayatollah Khomeini (right picture) became the leader of Iran. He ruled the country according to the Koran, the Islamic holy book. Until his death in 1989, he was the leader of a revival of Islamic fundamentalism.

142

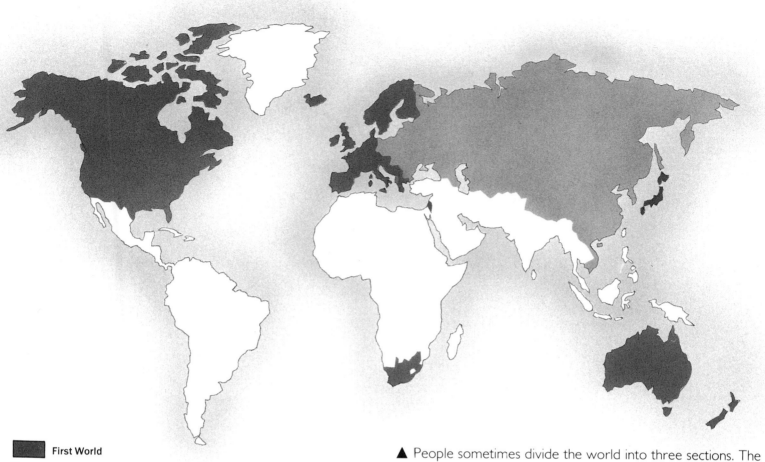

- First World
- Second World
- Third World

▲ People sometimes divide the world into three sections. The so-called First World, or 'developed market economies', contains the United States and its allies in Western Europe, the Far East and Australasia. The Second World, or 'centrally planned economies', consists of the Soviet Union, China and other communist states in Eastern Europe and Asia. The **Third World**, or 'developing market economies', includes most of Africa, Asia and South and Central America. However, many people dislike these labels because they are artificial and are based on economic wealth rather than the culture of the countries, and have been imposed by the richer countries on the poorer ones.

▼ Many parts of Africa have suffered crop failures, drought, floods and cyclones. In some countries, such as Mozambique (*below*), civil wars have led to the collapse of the national economy and food production. Such countries have become dependent for aid on Western countries.

▼ Many of the states in Central America are under the economic and political control of the United States. In 1979, a revolution in Nicaragua overthrew the American-supported ruler and replaced him with a popular government.

One world?

Over the last 200 years, the population of the world has risen—from about 600 million to more than five billion (5,000 million) in 1990. Some experts believe that by the year 2000 it will have risen to eight or ten billion. Of this huge population, two-thirds live in the Third World, in areas where poverty is so great that one in five children die before they reach their fifth birthday and most families lack decent food, housing, and medical attention.

Poverty is not the only problem facing the world today. During the 1980s, scientists have become more aware that human actions are harming our planet Earth. Industrial pollution and the exploitation of the world's natural resources are destroying irreplaceable plant and animal life and harming the delicate structure of the atmosphere. Disasters such as the industrial accident at Bhopal, in India, in which at least 2500 people were killed by poisonous gas in 1984 alerted people to the dangers of our modern world.

We are now more aware than ever that what happens in one part of the world has a direct effect on the rest of the world. This awareness has led to the formation of groups like Friends of the Earth and Greenpeace, whose aims are to protect the people, animals and plant life of our planet and ensure that future generations will be able to enjoy the world we live in today.

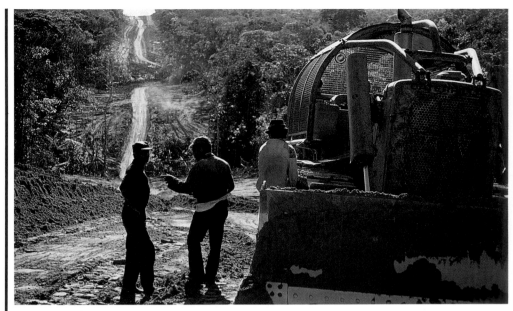

▲ Clearing the rainforest for the trans-American highway. Since the Second World War more than half of the world's rainforest has been cut down, destroying thousands of species of plants and animals.

▼ In 1984, a famine broke out in Ethiopia. The Irish singer Bob Geldorf arranged a huge international rock concert to raise money for the starving peoples. The Band Aid project sent food and other supplies to Ethiopia, as well as technical expertise to help the Ethiopians.

▶ Children in Oman learning about the wildlife of their country. All over the world people are becoming more aware of the need to conserve the Earth's natural resources.

144

Glossary

Words in this book in **bold** are explained in the Glossary below.

Absolute monarch A ruler such as Louis the Fourteenth who was completely responsible for governing a country.

Agriculture The science of raising animals and growing crops.

Alliance A friendly agreement between peoples, groups or countries.

Ambassador A person representing the interests of one country in another country.

Amphitheatre An oval or circular open-air theatre with seats around a central space.

Anthropology The scientific study of human beings.

Apartheid The policy of racial segregation pursued in South Africa.

Aqueduct A bridge built to carry water.

Arable land Land which is ploughed for growing crops.

Archaeology The study of ancient buildings, tools and other remains.

Aristocracy The nobility or other privileged groups in a country.

Armada (means 'fleet of warships') Usually describing the Spanish Armada which, in 1588, sailed against England.

Arms Race Rivalry between countries to build up supplies of weapons and weaponry.

Aryan The name given to the Indo-European invaders of India.

Astrolabe An instrument for measuring the height of the stars above sea level. It was used by early navigators and sailors.

Authoritarian Expecting total obedience.

Balance of power A situation when two or more nations are equal in power.

Bantu (means 'people') A group of people from central and southern Africa who speak one of the Bantu languages.

Barbarians A term used by the Romans to describe the nomadic invaders of their empire.

Baron A powerful landowner whose lands were given by the king.

Bourgeoisie The professional classes in society, such as teachers and lawyers.

Bronze An alloy (mixture) of copper and tin.

Caliph Religious ruler of a Muslim country.

Capitalism An economic system in which goods are produced for profit and investment is provided by a small group of people.

Caribs The original peoples of the Caribbean.

Caste A group of people within the Hindu religion considered to have the same social status or class.

Citadel An elevated fortress protecting a city.

Citizen A person who lives in a town or city.

City-state A city that is also an independent country.

Civilization A developed and settled way of life including living in towns or cities.

Civil War A war between different groups of people within one country.

Claimant A person who has a claim to the throne.

Cold War Hostility between two countries that does not result in actual fighting.

Colony A settlement abroad which is ruled or governed by another country. Colonists are people who leave their home country to live in a colony.

Commerce Trade or buying or selling.

Common land A large piece of land, that can be used by anyone.

Communism An economic and political system in which the state owns all property and means of production.

Conquistador (means 'conqueror') The name given to the Spanish adventurers who sailed to South America in search of gold and riches.

Consul One of the two Ancient Roman officials elected each year.

Convict A person convicted or found guilty of being a criminal.

Crusade Military expedition launched from Europe to recover the Holy Land from Muslim rule.

Culture Art, literature, music and painting. Culture is also used to describe the way of life of the people of a country or region.

Democracy A country in which the government is chosen by the people.

Dictator An unelected head of state who rules a country by force.

Dynasty A ruling family or series of rulers from one family.

Economy The financial and business affairs of a country.

Empire A group of countries under one ruler.

Excommunicate To expel someone from the Church.

Fascism A political system in which all power is concentrated in a strong, centralized state led by a dictator.

Feudal System A system of government based on land ownership and allegiance to the lord of the manor, the baron or the king.

Fossils Remains of ancient plants or animals, preserved as stone.

French Revolution The Revolution in France against the royal family (1789–95).

General Strike A refusal to work by employees in every trade in one country until certain demands are met.

Glacials Periods when large areas of Earth were covered by ice: ice ages.

Guild An association of workers sharing the same skill who join together to protect their interests and train new members.

Habsburgs The ruling house of Austria from the 1200s to the early 1900s.

Hieroglyphs Writing using picture symbols.

Hominid A member of the family *Hominidae*, which includes modern humans and their ancestors.

Immunity The body's natural defence against disease.

Independence Self-government for a colony.

Indigenous A word used to describe the native peoples of a country.

Interglacials The warmer periods between glacials.

Irrigation A method of supplying dry land with water so that crops can grow.

Islam The religion of the Arabs and other peoples who worship Allah and follow Muhammad as his prophet. Followers of Islam are known as Muslims.

Junk Chinese sailing boat used to transport goods.

Kiln A furnace used for firing pottery.

Kingdom A country ruled by a king or queen.

Land bridge A strip of land connecting two larger areas.

Maize A type of corn.

Maroons Peoples of the Caribbean who are of mixed Caribbean and African origin.

Merchant economy This term is used to describe an economy based on trade.

Mesoamerica A term for Mexico and Central America.

Minuscule Writing developed by scholars working for Charlemagne around 800.

Missionary A religious person who goes to another country to convert people to their religion.

Monarchy A country ruled by a king or queen.

Mosaic A picture made up of numerous pieces of different coloured stone or glass set in a wall, floor or ceiling.

Nation A group of people under one government.

Nationalism Determination of a group of people to run their own affairs as a state or nation.

Neanderthals A group of early people who lived in Europe from about 1000,000 BC to 35,000 BC.

Netherlands The name given to the kingdom of Holland.

Neutral A country which refused to take sides in international disputes or join in international military alliances.

New World A term used by the Europeans to describe the Americas.

Nomads People who move with their herds or flocks of animals in search of grazing land.

Oracle The means of consulting the gods about the future, or asking for advice.

Pastoralists People who herd and graze flocks of animals.

Pasture Land covered with grass used for grazing cattle or sheep.

Patron A wealthy supporter, usually of the arts.

Pharaoh (means 'great house') The title of the king of Egypt.

Philosophy The study of the meaning of existence.

Pilgrim A person who journeys to a religious site to worship there.

Plantation A large estate or area of land planted with trees or one crop such as sugar beet, tea, tobacco or cotton.

Pope Before the Reformation in the 1500s, head of the Christian Church in western Europe and based in Rome.

Primates A group of animals that includes humans and monkeys.

Pueblo Town or village built by native Americans.

Renaissance (means 'rebirth') A period of European history from the 1400s to the 1600s when people rediscovered the learning and work of the Ancient Greeks and Romans.

Republic A country with an elected government but no royal family.

Revolution A total, sometimes violent, change of political or economic conditions and their replacement with a new system.

Saga A long story concerning legendary or historical figures and events, passed down by word of mouth from parent to child.

Satrapies Administrative areas in ancient Persia.

Seals Cylinders engraved with a device which leaves an impression on soft wax.

Semitic languages The group of languages which includes modern Arabic, Aramaic and Hebrew.

Senate A group of aristocrats in Rome who advised the consuls, or later the emperor.

Shogun Military ruler of Japan.

Silk Road The main land route between China and Europe. Camel trains walked along it carrying travellers and goods for trade.

Slavery The ownership of people as property.

Smelting The process of extracting metal by heating it to a high temperature.

Socialism A political system based on the belief that the people as a whole should own and control a country's wealth.

Spice Islands The islands of south-east Asia from where spices were exported to Europe.

State A country or part of a country which governs its own affairs.

Steppes The grassy plains of central Asia.

Superpower A nation that has power and influence throughout the world, based on its economic and military might.

Tax Money paid by people to a government for the administration of the country.

Technology The practical use of scientific discoveries and inventions.

Terracotta Unglazed, usually brownish-red pottery.

Third World A term sometimes used to describe developing market economies, in particular the poor countries of Africa, Asia, and South and Central America.

Tournament A mock battle to test the strength and skills of knights and prepare them for warfare.

Trade The process of buying and selling goods.

Treaty A written agreement between one or more countries.

Triangular trade The sea trade in slaves and goods in the 1600s and 1700s.

Tribe A group of people often descended from the same person or sharing the same language and culture.

Tropics The areas of land around the Equator.

Tsar A Russian word meaning 'emperor' used to describe the rulers of Russia.

Villein A peasant tied to the land and under the authority of the lord of the manor.

Vizier In Ancient Egypt the title of a chief minister or the governor of a province.

Warlord A military leader who governs a part of a country as if it is his own property.

Westernized A word used to describe countries or ways of life that have been influenced by the Western part of the world such as the United States or Europe.

World War A war fought between nations throughout the world.

Ziggurat A type of pyramid built in ancient Babylonia.

Europe	**Near East**	**Africa**
BC *c.*40,000 Last ice age *c.*33,000 Neanderthals die out *c.*20,000 Cave art flourishes in France & Spain *c.*2000 Minoans build Knossos in Crete *c.*1600 Beginning of Mycenean civilization in Greece *c.*1450 Destruction of Minoan civilization *c.*1100 Phoenician supremacy in the Mediterranean 900–750 Rise of city-states in Greece 776 First Olympic Games 753 Founding of Rome (traditional date) 481 Greeks defeat Persian invasion *c.*400 Athens rises to power in Greece 431–404 War between Athens & Sparta *c.*300 Rome rises to power in Italy 264–146 Punic wars between Rome & Carthage 27 Octavian becomes first Roman Emperor **AD** 330 City of Constantinople (Istanbul) founded 370 Huns from Asia invade Europe 395 Roman Empire divided in two	**BC** *c.*8000 First farming in Mesopotamia *c.*7000 Walls of Jericho built *c.*3500 Beginnings of Sumerian civilization *c.*3200 First writing in Sumeria 2360 Akkadian Empire founded by Sargon 1792–1750 Rule of Hammurabi, King of Babylon *c.*1500 Iron first smelted by the Hittites *c.*1200 Beginnings of Jewish religion *c.*1200 Israelites colonize Palestine *c.*721–705 Assyrian Empire at height of its power 586 Babylonian captivity of Jews *c.*500 Persian Empire at its height 334 Alexander the Great begins conquest of Persia **AD** *c.*30 Crucifixion of Jesus Christ 70 Romans destroy Jerusalem; *diaspora* (dispersal) of Jews begins 132 Jewish rebellion against Rome 226(–651) Sassanians rule Persian Empire 330 Capital of Roman Empire transferred to Constantinople (Istanbul)	**BC** *c.*40,000 Earliest specimens of modern humans (*Homo sapiens*) found in Africa *c.*5000 Farming introduced into northern Africa *c.*3200 First Dynasty in Egypt *c.*2800 Pyramids of Giza begun *c.*2685 Beginning of 'Old Kingdom' in Egypt *c.*2500 Sahara begins to dry out *c.*1570 Beginning of 'New Kingdom' in Egypt *c.*900 Kingdom of Kush becomes independent of Egypt *c.*900 Nok culture of Nigeria begins 814 Phoenicians found colony at Carthage *c.*600 Iron smelting developed in northern Africa *c.*600 Bantu people move into southern Africa *c.*550 Arabs from Yemen colonize Ethiopia 332 Alexander the Great conquers Egypt **AD** 30 Egypt becomes a Roman province 350 Kingdom of Axum (Ethiopia) conquers Kush 350 Christianity reaches Ethiopia 429(–535) Vandal Kingdom in northern Africa

Asia & the Far East	**The Americas**	**Australasia**

Asia & the Far East	The Americas	Australasia
BC	**BC** *c.*40,000 First people migrate to America	**BC** *c.*50,000 First Aborigines arrive in Greater Australia
*c.*6000 Rice cultivated in Thailand	*c.*15,000 Cave art practised in Brazil	*c.*2000 First settlers arrive in New Guinea
*c.*2500–1500 Indus valley civilization	*c.*9000–7000 Flint arrowheads ('Folsom points') made in southern USA	*c.*1300 First settlers arrive in Fiji, Tonga & Samoa
*c.*1500 Shang Dynasty in China	*c.*4500 Farming develops in central America	
1028 Chou Dynasty in China	3372 First date in Mayan calendar	
*c.*650 Introduction of iron working	*c.*1500 Stone temples built in Mesoamerica	
563 Birth of the Buddha	*c.*1000 Chavín people of Peru making pottery	
551 Birth of Confucius	*c.*700 Stone city of Chavín de Huántar built	
	*c.*500 Gallinazo & Salinar cultures flourish in Peru	
320–184 Mauryan Dynasty rules northern India		
273–232 Asoka introduces Buddhism into southern India		
221 Ch'in Dynasty in China		
214 Great Wall of China completed		
202 Han Dynasty in China		
AD	**AD**	**AD**
50BC–AD50 Buddhism introduced into China	*c.*100 Olmec civilization flourishes in Mesoamerica	*c.*300 First settlers arrive in Polynesia
220(–587) Civil war in China (Six Dynasties period)	*c.*200 Hopewell Indians build burial mounds in Ohio	
320(–500) Gupta Dynasty rules northern India	*c.*300 Risa of Mayan civilization of Mesoamerica	
360–390 Japanese conquer Korea	*c.*500 Inuit begin hunting seals & whales	

Europe	**The Middle East**	**Africa**

Europe	The Middle East	Africa
452 Attila the Hun enters Italy. **455** Rome sacked by the Vandals. **476** The last Roman Emperor is overthrown. **527–65** Justinian attempts to recover the old Roman Empire for the Byzantine Empire. **711** Muslims invade Spain. **732** Muslim armies defeated in France at Poitiers. *c.***750** The Feudal System starts to emerge. **771–814** Charlemagne rules vast Frankish Empire in western Europe. **793** Vikings start to raid Britain and France. **843, 870** Charlemagne's empire split into three parts. **962** Otto the First of Germany is crowned as the first Holy Roman Emperor. **1066** Normans invade and conquer England. **1154** Angevin Empire of England and France reaches its greatest extent. **1237** Mongols invade Russia, Hungary and Poland. **1241** Hamburg and Lübeck set up a trading association, leading to the formation of the Hanseatic League. **1337–1453** Hundred Years' War between England and France. **1347–53** Black Death sweeps Europe.	**484** The Huns attack Persia and kill the Emperor. **527–65** Under Justinian, the Byzantine Empire conquers much of the Middle East. **579** At the end of the reign of Chosroes the First, the Sassanian Empire of Persia reaches its greatest extent. **622** Muhammad flees from Mecca to Medina. **630** Muhammad returns to Mecca and makes it the capital of his new empire. **632** Death of Muhammad and the start of Arab expansion throughout the Middle East. **642** The Arabs conquer Persia and overthrow the Sassanian Empire. **756** The Islamic Empire starts to break up into independent countries. **762** Baghdad is founded by Al-Mansur. **1096–9** The First Crusade captures Jerusalem and establishes a number of Christian states in the area. **1187** Jerusalem is recaptured from the Crusaders. **1258** The Mongols capture Baghdad. **1261** The Mongol advance in the Middle East is stopped by the Egyptians. **1291** The Crusaders are finally thrown out of the Holy Land.	**400** Axum in Ethiopia converts to Christianity. **429** The Vandals overrun the Roman Empire in north Africa and set up their own kingdom. **535** The Byzantine Emperor Justinian conquers north Africa. **639** Arabs invade Egypt. *c.***700** Whole of north Africa is now controlled by Arabs and converts to Islam. *c.***700** Arab traders start to cross the Sahara and trade with the peoples to the south. **700–1200** Kingdom of Ghana, the first great African empire, grows rich on trade. **971** World's first university is founded in Cairo. **1071** East African ports of Kilwa and Gedi send ambassadors to China. **1190** Lalibela becomes king of Ethiopia and starts to build new churches. **1235** The Kingdom of Mali is established. *c.***1250** The city of Jenne is founded. *c.***1300** Great Zimbabwe emerges as a major trading empire. **1324** Mansa Musa, king of Mali, goes on a pilgrimage to Mecca and astounds everyone with his wealth. **1418, 1422** Chinese fleets visit east Africa in search of trade.

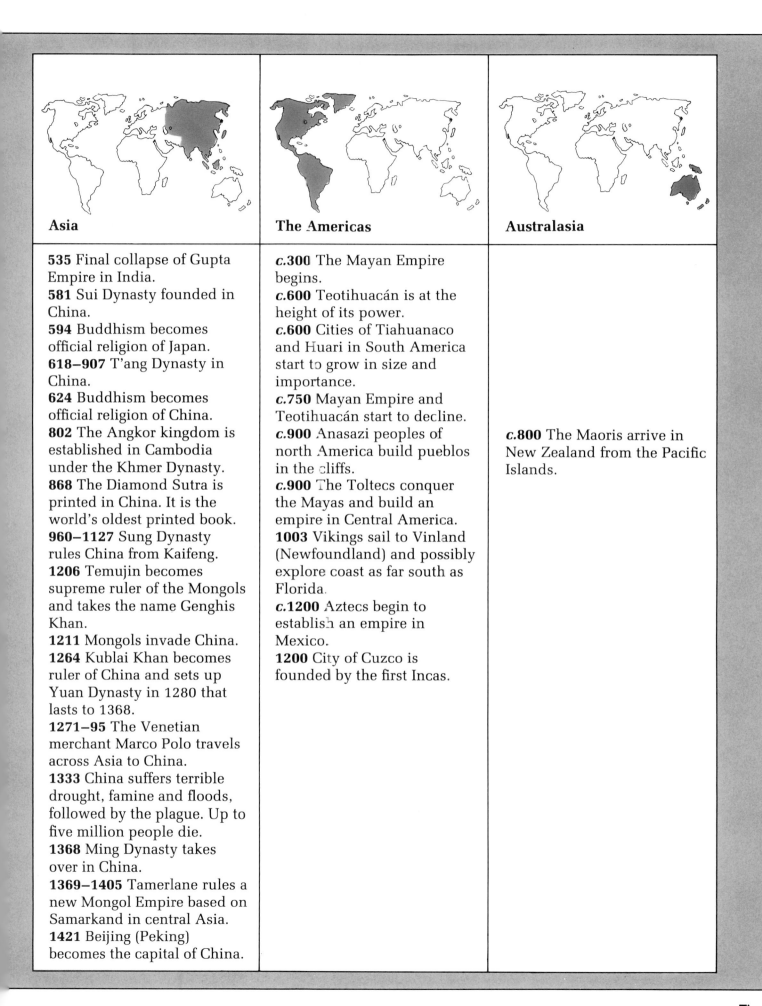

Asia

535 Final collapse of Gupta Empire in India.
581 Sui Dynasty founded in China.
594 Buddhism becomes official religion of Japan.
618–907 T'ang Dynasty in China.
624 Buddhism becomes official religion of China.
802 The Angkor kingdom is established in Cambodia under the Khmer Dynasty.
868 The Diamond Sutra is printed in China. It is the world's oldest printed book.
960–1127 Sung Dynasty rules China from Kaifeng.
1206 Temujin becomes supreme ruler of the Mongols and takes the name Genghis Khan.
1211 Mongols invade China.
1264 Kublai Khan becomes ruler of China and sets up Yuan Dynasty in 1280 that lasts to 1368.
1271–95 The Venetian merchant Marco Polo travels across Asia to China.
1333 China suffers terrible drought, famine and floods, followed by the plague. Up to five million people die.
1368 Ming Dynasty takes over in China.
1369–1405 Tamerlane rules a new Mongol Empire based on Samarkand in central Asia.
1421 Beijing (Peking) becomes the capital of China.

The Americas

*c.***300** The Mayan Empire begins.
*c.***600** Teotihuacán is at the height of its power.
*c.***600** Cities of Tiahuanaco and Huari in South America start to grow in size and importance.
*c.***750** Mayan Empire and Teotihuacán start to decline.
*c.***900** Anasazi peoples of north America build pueblos in the cliffs.
*c.***900** The Toltecs conquer the Mayas and build an empire in Central America.
1003 Vikings sail to Vinland (Newfoundland) and possibly explore coast as far south as Florida.
*c.***1200** Aztecs begin to establish an empire in Mexico.
1200 City of Cuzco is founded by the first Incas.

Australasia

*c.***800** The Maoris arrive in New Zealand from the Pacific Islands.

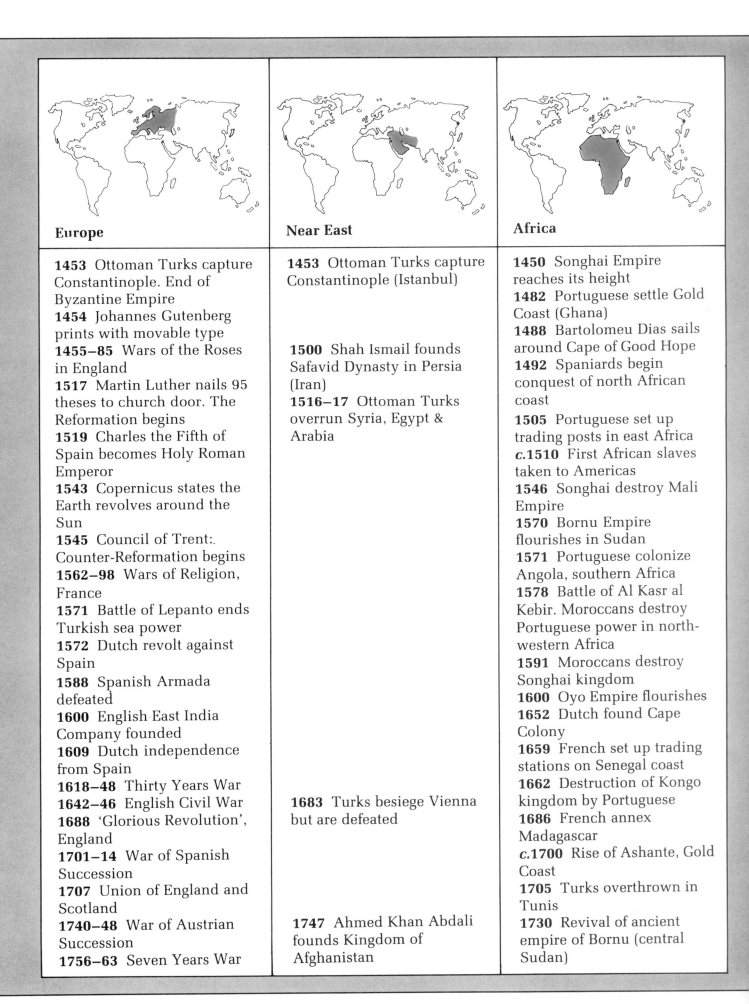

Europe	Near East	Africa

1453 Ottoman Turks capture Constantinople. End of Byzantine Empire
1454 Johannes Gutenberg prints with movable type
1455–85 Wars of the Roses in England
1517 Martin Luther nails 95 theses to church door. The Reformation begins
1519 Charles the Fifth of Spain becomes Holy Roman Emperor
1543 Copernicus states the Earth revolves around the Sun
1545 Council of Trent: Counter-Reformation begins
1562–98 Wars of Religion, France
1571 Battle of Lepanto ends Turkish sea power
1572 Dutch revolt against Spain
1588 Spanish Armada defeated
1600 English East India Company founded
1609 Dutch independence from Spain
1618–48 Thirty Years War
1642–46 English Civil War
1688 'Glorious Revolution', England
1701–14 War of Spanish Succession
1707 Union of England and Scotland
1740–48 War of Austrian Succession
1756–63 Seven Years War

1453 Ottoman Turks capture Constantinople (Istanbul)

1500 Shah Ismail founds Safavid Dynasty in Persia (Iran)
1516–17 Ottoman Turks overrun Syria, Egypt & Arabia

1683 Turks besiege Vienna but are defeated

1747 Ahmed Khan Abdali founds Kingdom of Afghanistan

1450 Songhai Empire reaches its height
1482 Portuguese settle Gold Coast (Ghana)
1488 Bartolomeu Dias sails around Cape of Good Hope
1492 Spaniards begin conquest of north African coast
1505 Portuguese set up trading posts in east Africa
*c.***1510** First African slaves taken to Americas
1546 Songhai destroy Mali Empire
1570 Bornu Empire flourishes in Sudan
1571 Portuguese colonize Angola, southern Africa
1578 Battle of Al Kasr al Kebir. Moroccans destroy Portuguese power in north-western Africa
1591 Moroccans destroy Songhai kingdom
1600 Oyo Empire flourishes
1652 Dutch found Cape Colony
1659 French set up trading stations on Senegal coast
1662 Destruction of Kongo kingdom by Portuguese
1686 French annex Madagascar
*c.***1700** Rise of Ashante, Gold Coast
1705 Turks overthrown in Tunis
1730 Revival of ancient empire of Bornu (central Sudan)

		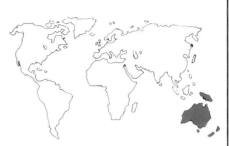
Asia & the Far East	**The Americas**	**Australasia**

Asia & the Far East	The Americas	Australasia
1471 Vietnamese expand southwards	**1438** Inca Empire established, Peru	
1498 Vasco da Gama reaches India via Cape of Good Hope	**1440–69** Montezuma rules Aztec Empire	
1519 Nanak founds Sikh religion in India	**1492** Columbus reaches Carribean	
1526 Babur conquers Delhi and founds Mughal Empire	**1494** Treaty of Tordesillas divides Americas between Portugal and Spain	
1550 Mongol Altan Khan invades northern China	**1497** Cabot reaches Newfoundland	
1592–3, 1597–8 Japan invades Korea but is expelled by China	**1520** Magellan crosses Pacific Ocean	
c.1608 Tokugawa period begins in Japan	**1521** Cortés conquers Aztec capital Tenóchtitlán	
1608 Confucianism becomes official religion in Japan	**1533** Pizarro conquers Peru	
1619 Portuguese found Batavia (Jakarta)	**1545** Discovery of silver mines in Peru and Mexico	
1630s Japan isolates itself from the rest of the world	**c.1560** Portuguese set up sugar plantations in Brazil	
1644 Manchus found Ch'in Dynasty, China	**1607** First English settlement in America (Jamestown, Virginia)	
1648 Taj Mahal completed, India	**1608** French colonists found Quebec	
1649 Russians reach Pacific and found Okhotsk	**1620** Puritans on *Mayflower* land in New England	
1690 Calcutta founded by British in India	**1624** Dutch settle New Amsterdam	
c.1690 Russia expands to Black Sea	**1636** Harvard College founded – first university in America	**1642** Tasman reaches New Zealand and Tasmania
1697 Chinese occupy Outer Mongolia	**1664** British seize New Amsterdam, re-name it New York	
1707 Death of Aurangzeb, decline of Mughal Empire, India	**1684** La Salle explores Mississippi. Claims Louisiana for France	
1708 Sikhs rule Punjab		
1720 Manchus rule in Tibet	**1728** Bering explores Alaska	
1736 Nader Shah deposes Safavid Dynasty	**1759** British capture Quebec from French.	**1768** James Cook explores Pacific
1751 China overruns Tibet		

Europe	Near East	Africa

Europe

1760s Industrial Revolution starts in Britain.
1762–96 Catherine the Great rules Russia.
1789 French Revolution starts.
1792 French declare republic and execute king in 1793.
1799 Napoleon takes power in France.
1815 Napoleon defeated by British at Waterloo. The French monarchy is restored.
1848 Revolutions break out across Europe.
1861–70 Italy is united.
1871 Germany is united.
1914–18 First World War.
1917 Russian Revolution.
1919 Treaty of Versailles establishes new countries in Eastern Europe.
1922 Ireland becomes independent from Britain.
1933 Hitler takes power in Germany.
1936–9 Spanish Civil War.
1939–45 Second World War.
1948 Communist governments take power in Eastern Europe.
1949 NATO and Warsaw Pact.
1957 Treaty of Rome establishes Common Market.
1968 Russian troops invade Czechoslovakia.
1989/90 Popular pro-democracy uprisings throughout Eastern Europe.
1990 Germany is reunited. Mrs Thatcher resigns as British prime minister.

Near East

1760 Ottoman Turks rule most of Near East.
1820 Britain establishes control in Persian Gulf states.
1908 Revolution in Turkey.
1914–18 First World War.
1917 Britain issues Balfour Declaration promising a Jewish homeland in Palestine.
1918 Ottoman Empire collapses: Iraq becomes independent.
1922 Turkish Republic established under Atatürk.
1922 Syria and Lebanon under French control, Palestine and Jordan under British control.
1932 Saudi Arabia united.
1939–45 Second World War.
1943 Syria and Lebanon become independent.
1946 Jordan independent.
1947–8 Palestine is partitioned and the Jewish state of Israel is set up.
1948 Arab–Israeli War.
1956 Egyptian take-over of Suez Canal leads to Israeli invasion and British–French occupation of Canal.
1967 Six Day Arab–Israeli War.
1973 Yom Kippur Arab–Israeli War.
1974– Civil War in Lebanon.
1979 Peace Treaty between Egypt and Israel.
1980–88 Iran–Iraq War.
1990 Iraq invades Kuwait – the 'Gulf Crisis'.

Africa

1795 Britain acquires Cape of Good Hope from the Dutch.
1822 USA establishes Liberia as an independent state for freed slaves.
1830 France invades Algeria.
1835–7 Dutch settlers (Boers) leave Cape Colony in Great Trek inland.
1842–3 War between Boers and British.
1869 Suez Canal opened.
1880s Africa divided up by European powers.
1899–1902 Boer War between Britain and Boers.
1910 South Africa becomes independent state in British Empire.
1914–18 First World War.
1935 Italy invades Ethiopia.
1939–45 Second World War.
1954–62 Civil War in Algeria leads to French withdrawal and Algerian independence.
1957 Ghana receives its independence from Britain.
1960 French African colonies become independent.
1975 Portugal declares all its African colonies independent.
1980 Zimbabwe is the last British colony in Africa to receive its independence.
1989 Open elections in Namibia, south-west Africa.
1990 Nelson Mandela released from prison. Namibia gains independence.

Asia

The Americas

Australasia

1763 Britain establishes control over India.
1839–42 Trade War between China and Britain.
1853 USA forces Japan to trade with foreigners.
1857–8 Indian Mutiny against British rule.
1861 France establishes first colonies in Indo-China.
1868 Japan starts to modernize.
1900 Boxer Rebellion against foreign influence in China.
1904–5 Russian–Japanese War; Japan controls Korea.
1911 Chinese Revolution leads to overthrow of Manchu Dynasty and establishment of republic.
1914–18 First World War.
1927 Start of Chinese Civil War.
1931 Japanese begin conquest of China.
1939–45 Second World War
1946–54 War against French control of Indo-China.
1947 India and Pakistan gain independence from Britain.
1949 Dutch grant independence to Indonesia.
1949 Communist Party takes control in China.
1950–3 Korean War.
1954–73 Vietnam War leads to union of Vietnam in 1975.
1989 Pro-democracy movement in Beijing, China is severely repressed.
1990 Pro-democracy demonstrations in Nepal.

1763 Britain gains complete control of Canada; acquires other colonies in America.
1775–83 American Revolution.
1776 American colonies declare their independence.
1783 United States formed.
1789 George Washington is first president of USA.
1804 Haiti becomes independent after successful slave revolt.
1808–25 Spanish and Portuguese colonies in South and Central America fight for their independence.
1861–5 American Civil War.
1867 Alaska is bought by USA from Russia.
1867 Canada becomes independent from Britain.
1869 Railway link across USA.
1914 Panama Canal opens.
1917 USA declares war on Germany.
1929 Wall Street crash leads to Great Depression.
1932–45 F. D. Roosevelt becomes US president.
1941 USA enters Second World War.
1945 United Nations Organisation founded.
1963 US president John Kennedy assassinated.
1968 US Civil rights leader Martin Luther King assassinated.
1987 USA signs INF Treaty with Soviet Union.

1768–79 Captain Cook explores the South Pacific and claims Australia for Britain.
1788 The first convicts arrive in Australia from Britain. Setting up of Botany Bay.
1840 New Zealand becomes a British colony.
1880s British, French and Germans colonize South Pacific.
1900 Hawaii becomes an American colony.
1901 Australia becomes an independent state in the British Empire.
1907 New Zealand becomes an independent state in the British Empire.
1914–18 First World War.
1920 Australia and Japan acquire former German colonies in the Pacific.
1927 Canberra becomes the federal capital of Australia.
1939–45 Second World War.
1941 Japanese bomb American naval base at Pearl Harbor, Hawaii, and bring USA into World War II.
1959 Hawaii becomes 50th member of the United States.
1970s Many British island colonies in South Pacific receive their independence.
1975 Papua New Guinea receives its independence from Australia.
1985 South Pacific Forum draws up the South Pacific Nuclear Free Zone Treaty.

Index

Page numbers in *italics* refer to illustrations

A

Aachen (Germany) 56
Aborigines 42, 78, 79, 110
Afghanistan 22, 69, 94
Africa: prehistoric 11; Ancient Empires 40–1; Roman Empire 44, 45; Carthage 47; Byzantine Empire 48; Islam 52; trade 66–7, 100; Benin, Kingdom of 78, 79, 101; Europeans in 82, 83, 86, 100, 101, 126–7; slaves 99, 100; independent cultures and states 101, 112, 142; South Africa 126, 127, 142
Africanus, Leo 101
agriculture: 'Fertile Crescent' 14, 15; Africa 40, 41, 100, 143; Egypt 18–20; China 24, 108; Japan 26; Indus valley 28; Phoenician 30; Athens 34; 'Mesoamerica' 38; feudal system 72–3; horse power 75; Aztec 84; Europe 90; agricultural revolution 114–15; USA 135
aircraft 131
Akkadian Empire 17
Al-Mansur 53
Alexander the Great 22, 29
Alexandria 45
Alfred, King 58
Americas, the :Early peoples 12, 38–9, 44, 53, 64–5, 78; European exploration 82, 83, 84–6; slaves 99; colonies 112, 116, 119; US influences 143; rainforests 144, *see also* United States of America
amphitheatres 35
Amritsar, Golden Temple at *94*
Angles 47
apartheid 142
aqueducts 35
Arabs 49, 52, 53, 58, 62; in Africa 66, 67; Arab-Israeli conflict 137, 142
archaeology 10
Arctic region 39
Argentina 119
Armada 86
Armstrong, Neil *139*
Aryans 28, 29
Asia 68–9, 82; early civilizations 24–9, *see also names of individual states*
Asoka, Kingdom of (India) 28, 54
Assyrians 16, 17, 23
astronomy 53, 64, 80, 84
Athenians *33*, 34
Atomic bombs 136, *137*

Augustus, Emperor of Rome 36
Australia 12, 42, 44, 53, 78, 79, 110, 126
Australopithecus 10, *11*
Austria 69, 102, 104, 122, 123, 130, 132, 134, 136
Avars 56
Axum, kingdom of 45
Aztec Empire 44, 64, 78, 84–5

B

Babur (Mughal Emperor) 94, *95*
Babylonia 16, 17
Baghdad 53, 68
banks 72, 90
Bantu peoples 40
Barbarians 46–7
barley *14*, 20
barons 61, 72
Bastille fortress 117
Batavia (Jakarta) 87
Bayeux Tapestry *60*
Beatles *141*
beer *20*
Beijing 68, 112, *113*, 140
Belgium 122, 126
Benin, Kingdom of 78, 79, 101
Berlin Wall *137*
Bessemer, Henry 121
Bhopal disaster 144
bicycles *131*
Black Death *71*
boats: *see* water transport
Boers 127
Bolívar, Simon *119*
Bolsheviks 133
Book of Kells (manuscript) *51*
books 51, 52, 56, 60, 68, 75, 81, 105
Borgia, Lucrezia 91
Borobudur (Java) *54*
Boston Tea Party *116*
'Boxer' rebellion *128*
bread-making *34*
Britain: early Britain 35, 47, 50, 58, 59; Normans 60–1; English Parliament 70; Peasants' Revolt 71; colonies/Empire 86, 94, 95, 96–8, 99, 100, 110, 112, 116, 118, 124, 126, 127, 135; church 88, 89, 97; agriculture 90, 114; political reform 91, 122, 130; women's rights 91, 130; English Civil War 102; industry 114–15, 120–1; World Wars 130, 132, 136
British East India Company 95
bronze 25, 26, 32, 33, 79, 101
Buddhism 24, 27, 29, 50, 54–5
Bulgars 48
Burma 54, 136, 137
Byzantine Empire 48–9, 52

C

Cabot, John *83*
Cairo 53

Canada 58, 96, 98, 104
canals 104, 114, 127
Canton *128*
caravans (desert) 67
caravels (ships) *82*
Caribbean 82, 83, 84, 86, 96, 99, 112, 119
Carolingian Dynasty 56
Carthage 30, 47
Cartier, Jacques 96
carvings *see* sculpture
caste system, Hindu 54
castles 60, *61*, 62
Çatal Hüyük 15
cathedrals *72*
Catherine of Aragon 89
Catherine de Medici 89
Catherine the Great *113*
cave art *12*, *13*
Cavour, Count 122
Central America 84, 96, 112, 119, 143, *see also* Aztec Empire; Mexico
Ceylon (Sri Lanka) 86, 137
Charlemagne 56
Charles the First, King of England 102
Charles the Second, King of England 102
Charles the Second, King of Spain 102
Chartists *122*
Cheng Ho *83*
Chiang Kai-shek 140
child labour 114, *121*
Children's Crusade 62
Chile 119
China 21, 24–6, 27, 44, 45, 46, 50; Buddhism 54–5; and Europeans 57, 76, 112, 128; trade with Africa 66, 67; Mongols 68; inventions 75; cities 76; Ming Dynasty 78, 79, 83, 108–9; Communists 122, 140; wars 136, 138, 139
china (porcelain) *108*
Christianity 37, 46, 48, 50–1, 67, 70, 72, 88–9; Crusades 62–3; Quakers 91; Puritans 97, 102
Churchill, Winston *137*
cinema *134*
city-states 16, 34, 64, 70
cloth/clothing 16, 19, 20, 24, 29, 30, 32, 100; China 55; Samurai 109; Japan 129
Clovis (Frankish king) 56
coal 114, 115, *120*
Colosseum (Rome) *35*
Columbus, Christopher 58, 82, 83
Common Market 142
Communism 122, 133, 140
concentration camps *136*
Confucianism 24, 27
conquistadors 84, 90
Constantine, Emperor 48, 50
Constantinople *48*, 62, 82, 92, *93*
Cook, James 110

Acknowledgements

The publishers wish to thank the following for supplying photographs for this book:

Ancient Art and Architecture Collection 13, 17 (bottom), 29 (bottom), 34 (bottom), 36 (middle and bottom), 76 (top), 88; Ashmolean Museum 58; Associated Press 139 (bottom right), 140 (bottom), 141 (bottom right), 142, 143 (left); Band Aid 144 (middle); The Bettmann Archive 123 (right); Bibliothèque Nationale 48 Ms Lat 4825 f37v; Bodleian Library 53 (top) Ms Marsh 144f.61; (left) Ms Lococke 37s f3v4r, 63 Ms Douce 195 fol. 7, 68 (bottom) Ms Bodley 264 fol. 237, 93 (top left); Bridgeman Art Library 118, 119 (left); British Library 72 (top), Ms Add 27695 fol. 8, 75 (top), 98 (bottom), 110 (top), 116 (top); British Museum 22, 43, 52 (middle), 68 (top), 85 (bottom), 97 (top right), 100 (top right); Camera Press 135 (left), 137, 138; Ekdotike Athenon 33 (left), Mary Evans Picture Library 93, 99 (bottom), 105 (bottom), 109 (bottom left), 115 (middle), 117, 119 (right), 121 (right), 122 (right), 123 (left), 127 (bottom), 128 (bottom), 130, 131 (left); Fitzwilliam Museum, Cambridge 19 (bottom); Fotomas Index 106 (top and bottom), 108, 110 (bottom); Courtesy, French Government Tourist Office 12; Giraudon 75 (bottom), 104 (bottom); Grisewood and Dempsey Ltd 121 (bottom); Sonia Halliday Photographs 14 (top), 15, 23 (top), 30, 36 (top), 37, 45, 49, 57, 62, 93 (top right); Robert Harding Picture Library 55 (top), Barbara Heller 67 (bottom); Michael Holford 10 (bottom), 19 (top right), 27, 33 (right), 34 (top), 35 (right), 47, 60 (top), 65 (bottom), 77, 80, 82, 95 (bottom left), 106 (middle), 109 (top); Hulton-Deutsch Collection 101, 109 (bottom right), 127 (top); Hulton-Deutsch Collection 115 (bottom right), 122, 123 (bottom), 125, 129 (top), 134 (bottom), 135 (top); The Hutchison Library 10 (top), 23 (bottom), 25, 35 (left), 38 (top), 41, 42, 54, 67, 69, 79, 139 (bottom left), 141 (middle), 143 (right), 144 (top); ICCE Photolibrary/Mark Boulton 144 (bottom); The Imperial War Museum 132, 136; The David King Collection 133 (bottom), 140 (top); The Kobal Collection 134 (top); The Library of Congress 124; The Mansell Collection 55 (right), 70, 73 (top), 74, 81, 87, 89 (bottom), 98 (top), 103 (bottom), 120, 128 (top), 131 (right); Museum of Athens 32 (top), Museum of the American Indian, Heye Foundation 39 (top); NASA 39 (middle left); NRSC Library 111, 129 (middle right); National Bibliothek, Vienna 9, 72 (bottom), 73 (bottom); National Maritime Museum 86 (bottom); Peter Newark's Pictures 85 (top), 97 (top left and bottom), 99 (right), 100 (top left), 116 (bottom), 135 (right); Novosti 133 (top); Picturepoint 105 (top); Popperfoto 141 (bottom left); Punch Library 126; Ann Ronan Picture Library 103 (top), 121 (left); SCALA 46, 50, 71; Courtesy, Sir John Soane's Museum 61; Society for Cultural Relations with U.S.S.R. 139 (top); South American Pictures 65 (top), 84; Spectrum Colour Library 19 (top left), 26, 32 (bottom); Straatliche Museum, Berlin 14 (bottom); Trinity College, Cambridge 51 (left); Trinity College, Dublin 51 (right), Universitets Oldsaksamlung 59 (right); Vienna Art History Museum 90; The Wallace Collection 104 (top); Werner Forman Archive 38 (top), 39 (bottom), 53 (right), 59 (left), 76 (bottom), 86 (top), 95 (top), 100 (bottom); ZEFA 17 (top), 29 (top), 52 (top), 55 (left), 64, 66, 89 (top), 93 (bottom), 94, 95 (bottom right), 107, 141 (top).